Costume Reference 1

Roman Britain
and the
Middle Ages

MARION SICHEL

Publishers   PLAYS, INC.   *Boston*

First published 1977
© text and illustrations 1977, Marion Sichel

First American edition published by Plays, Inc. 1977

Library of Congress Cataloging in Publication Data

Sichel, Marion.
    Costume Reference.
      Includes bibliographies and indexes.
CONTENTS: v. 1 Roman Britain and the Middle Ages –
v. 2 Tudors and Elizabethans.
1. Costume – Great Britain – History.
I. Title
GT 730.S48   1977   391'.00941
76-54466   0-8238-0211-6 (vol. 1)

Printed in Great Britain

Contents

Introduction

During the period of the Roman occupation, English fashion showed a great development in style. The Romans brought more advanced methods of weaving and decoration, which increased further the styles of barbaric culture.

After the Romans' withdrawal, the Celts retained some of the Roman culture. This, however, was partially destroyed by the new invasions and settlements from Europe, notably of the Danish and Saxon conquests.

By the tenth century Britain had developed its own style and fashion. English women were renowned throughout Europe for their skills in embroidery during this period. Garments for both male and female showed only minor differences, being simple tunics, cloaks, headdresses and decorations.

After the Norman conquest in 1066, French influence on fashion became apparent. With travelling merchants, commerce became easier, and richer and finer materials replaced the home-spuns. The Norman Crusaders brought back Eastern riches which gave wider scope to fashion.

Norman craftsmen had seen the work of the Syrians and the new ideas were used in the making of jewellery as well as designs on belts, shoes, buckles and other accessories.

Norman architecture was reflected in the style of clothes worn. The square towers of the Norman churches were parallel to the short, conical headdress worn by the soldiers of the period. They shared the same sense of the functional and forceful. As the Normans fought a great deal, much armour was worn by the men. When not fighting, they wore long loose gowns, which were often fur-lined as Norman dwellings were cold.

Ladies' clothes were still ground length and sometimes trailed behind. The Norman ladies, richer than the Saxons, wore clothes made of richer materials and jewellery.

The toe shapes of the shoes were not yet pointed, and like the Norman character, were rather blunt. The Moors of Spain supplied England and the rest of Europe with a leather called *Cordoba*, from which the word 'cordwainer' originated, a beautiful soft leather, mainly in red and used for shoe-making.

In the Plantagenet period, buildings were perpendicular in design. The tall, pointed steeples were reproduced in the tall, pointed, hennin headdress worn by the women. The tall, slender steeples of the cathedrals were echoed in the long, slender cuffs of the sleeves and the matching long points to the hoods called *liripipes*.

During the reign of King John (1199–1216) colour became an important factor in fashion. Shoes were made of fabrics or leather, being dyed in various colours, either matching or in contrast to the colours of the clothes. They were also very elaborate in design with the toes reaching extreme lengths. Poorer people wore the same styles as the rich, but they were less ornate and remained in neutral colours.

The female profile in the twelfth century, was that of rounded breasts and wide hips, whereas in the thirteenth century the breasts were higher and the waist more pronounced. Dresses also gradually became longer and were draped so that the figure was more pronounced.

More under-garments were now worn. A short bodice was worn between the *chainse*, a linen garment, and the *bliaud*, a long, close-fitting tunic. Small bands were worn to both hold and support the breasts. Made of linen or silk, these were worn over the chainse, and later became known as the chemise. A *gipon* which was a close-fitting waistcoat, was often worn over a dress, but was similar to a corset. Also worn was a blanchet, a long camisole which took its name from the colour *blanc*. A short tunic, called a *cote*, with wide sleeves and laced-up like a corset, was worn by the men. To emphasize the hips, the chemise had small pockets which were filled with wadding. These pads, like the lacing and the bands, all helped to emphasize and exaggerate the shape of the body.

In the medieval era women's clothes became longer and the layers of clothing increased. In this same period men's clothes became shorter and between the eleventh and the end

Early British Druid High-priest

5

of the fourteenth century, the masculine robe fell into decline. The varying kinds of braiers, braies and trunk hose gradually produced trousers. Thus men's and women's clothes began to differ.

Hose were made of thread or wool and held up by garters above knee level. Corsets became longer and were decorated. By the fifteenth century shoulders were bared by the décolletage and dresses became so long that an iron hook, known as a *troussoir*, was attached to a cord from which the train hung. The chemise was usually made of transparent materials in yellow, gold and flesh colours.

During Edward III's reign (1327–1377) the hoods could be worn attached to the cloaks or capes. During this period fashion as we define it started to develop. Men's and women's fashions began to differ from each other increasingly; women's clothes became simpler with the greatest change in the headdresses. The *cote-hardie* or gown became close fitting with long tight sleeves, low and wide necklines, and hung full from the hips. Over this was worn the surcote or jacket of the thirteenth century, the sides of which were now cut away at the bodice so as to leave a broad piece of material of fur around the shoulders, the rest falling in panels at the front and back. These panels were joined to bands just below hip level from which a full skirt hung.

Elaborate headdresses and veils became fashionable after 1350. In the late Gothic period, from approximately 1350–1480, the vertical lines of the architecture was, possibly unconsciously, copied in the tall headdresses and long shoes Stained glass windows influenced the intricate cut-out vamps on shoes and other designs on clothes. The slender, delicate lines of the Plantagenets were gradually replaced by more square and horizontal lines.

Romano-British peasants

The Roman Influence

The pre-eminent dress of the Romans who occupied the British Isles was the *toga*, which distinguished them from the barbaric costume of the inhabitants of these islands. The toga was the Roman national dress and was worn by both male and female from the highest order to the lowest plebian. The toga remained fashionable until the last days of the Roman Empire.

Types of materials and colours, more than cut of design, distinguished the female from the male costume.

TOGAS

The toga was very large in size, being some three times the length of the body and twice the width of the wearer. It was cut as a square piece of material, on the round, or a mixture of both. It had one straight side and the other side was rounded off in a semi-circular style, showing that it could also have been cut on a semi-circular basis. Many methods have been suggested. The actual fitting is also in question; whether it draped the body by merely being thrown over in such a way as to fall into the required folds or was placed on the body by first being folded lengthwise about the middle, gathered into heavy folds, and then thrown over the left shoulder, which allowed about one-third of the length to hang down in front. The rest of the material was then passed in a diagonal direction across the back, drawn through under the right arm, and cast back over the left shoulder. Due to its width it hung over the left arm almost covering it. The finishing touch was to take the material which lay across the back and spread it out to cover the right shoulder. The corner piece, which hung forward over the left shoulder, was shortened by pulling the toga up at the chest and allowing it to fall over the heavy folds. The gathered group of folds at the chest was used as a pocket and was called the *sinus*.

It is also suggested that the toga could have been constructed by more intricate means in various component pieces, similar to a modern garment, then fastened together, although from the study of the art of the period no fastenings are visible. But the fact does remain that the toga followed a decided pattern with little or no variation in its division and folds. The general style or pattern of the toga, whether thrown or concocted, formed a short sleeve over the right arm which was left uncovered, the left arm being covered almost down to the wrist. The group of folds hung over the contoured drapery in front, the hanging folds being full enough at the back to allow the material to be drawn up to cover the head as was occasionally done during religious ceremonies and during inclement weather.

Togas were made from wool. Earlier garments retained their natural yellowish colour. Later variations of the toga were dyed various hues. The *toga sordida* was in black, this being the colour for mourning. Simple togas made from coarse wool were worn by the common people. Linen and silks were worn by the upper classes.

When the garment was edged with a border of purple, it was known as the *toga praetexta*. In this form it was worn by all youths of the nobility up to the age of fifteen, who also wore the *bulla*, a small round gold box suspended from the neck by means of an amulet, and resting on the chest. After this age the garment was changed for a toga without decorations and called a *toga pura* or *virilis*. Priests and judges also wore the toga praetexta as a mark of their profession. Knights wore a toga which was striped throughout with purple and this was called a *trabea*. For ceremonial and triumphal entries, generals wore a *coram populo*, which was a toga entirely of purple material and which was later embroidered with gold and then known as the *toga picta*.

TUNICS

The tunic, a copy of the Greek *chiton*, was worn by both sexes. It was used by upper classes as under-garments. Worn by the men, it reached halfway down the thigh; longer than this was considered effeminate, as longer lengths were worn only by women. Although worn at sacrificial ceremonies the tunic was worn only by the lower order and lesser functionaries without a toga (that being reserved by the candidates and others who continued to affect a display of humility). The tunic was made up of two pieces of material sewn together. It was put on over the head and pulled in at the waist by a belt. Soldiers and peasants wore it without a toga, as

Military buskin with lion's head decoration

8

The tailor-made figure-fitting armour for the higher ranks of the army followed the style of the Greeks. The cuirass or lorica followed the contours of the body, often being formed into muscle shapes. Engravings were very popular on both the cuirass and the shoulder plates. The body armour was in two parts, front and back, and was fastened by hinges. Either leather or metal straps hung from the waist and shoulders as protection. Under the armour was worn the short, knee-length tunica. The calf-length military buskin was made of leather with the heads and claws of animals as decoration.

This military type of toga was usually worn over armour and fastened on the right shoulder and called a 'paludamentum'. The back folds were drawn up and placed over the head in a hood fashion.

their sole garment. When it had wide sleeves attached it was called a *dalmatic*.

Senators wore their tunics edged with broad purple borders, known as *lati-clavus*. The knights were distinguished by a narrower border of purple called *angusti-clavus*.

Roman women wore over the under-tunic a long straight tunic, called a *stola*, which descended to the feet. It either hung straight down or assumed a variety of modifications with belts or girdles, and was made of a soft wool or linen. Over the stola was worn a *palla*. This was a voluminous cloak type of garment, similar to the toga but cut in a rectangular shape; it was folded lengthwise and held on each shoulder by a *fibula* or brooch.

Although still worn in the towns and cities, the toga was gradually superseded both in the country and the military by the Grecian *pallium* or mantle, which was considered to be less cumbersome than the trailing toga. The pallium when worn by soldiers over their armour was called a *paludamentum*, and was fastened on the right shoulder by a clasp or ornamental brooch. For travelling, the Romans wore a heavy woollen cape, a *paenula*, with a hood, a *cucullus*. The common people wore a hooded cloak, a *bacrocucullus*, made from a coarse, brown wool.

Short hair, frontal fringe.

HEAD–WEAR
Generally for males the head went uncovered with the hair worn short. Felt-type hats were worn on occasions, as was the rimless cap, the *pileus*, the wide-brimmed hat and the *Phrygian bonnet* were also worn.

In public, Roman women usually had their heads covered either by a veil or draped with the folds of the palla. Generally the hair was parted in the middle and drawn into a chignon at the nape of the neck; the hair was waved and surrounded the face with a frame of tight curls. Later hairdressing became more elaborate with such artificial aids as false hair pieces and wigs. Blond hair was very fashionable, so bleaching and wigs of this colour were used extensively. The simple headbands of the previous fashion were replaced by gold and silver nets encrusted with gems and precious stones. Precious metal tiaras were also worn.

Roman with short, curly hair and beard after the Emperor Hadrian.

FOOTWEAR
Sandals and shoes were made from leather and were produced in a great variety of shapes and styles for both male and

Hair shaped and curled, but clean-shaven.

Short, curly hair and beard.

Hair curled in front with curling irons.

female. Much of Roman footwear was copied from Greek fashions. Sandals and boots, some reaching to mid-calf, were worn, as were bootees or *calcei* with thongs fastening above the ankle. The *crepida*, a flat sandal made like a bootee with a filled-in heel-piece and low, leather side pieces, fastened with criss-cross thonging over the foot and tied at the ankle exposing the toes. *Soccus*, a two-piece sandal with a flat sole with two side straps closing between the first and second toes, and a white linen sock with divided toes for the toe-post in the sandal, was also popular. From this sandal comes the word 'sock'.

Later, shoes became more elaborate and were made from fine leathers. Brightly coloured dyes were used and decoration was added with gold, silver and precious stones.

ACCESSORIES

Beauty accessories were in abundance: face patches, powder, rouge and eyeblack were in common use. Employed for beauty aids were: combs, brushes, curling tongs, nets, hairpins, slides, mirrors, pomades, bleaches and dyes. Fans and umbrellas were carried by males and females.

Sandal with soft fold-over tab which concealed the fastening.

Sandal with strapping and cut out, laced over a high tongue which covered the entire front of the foot.

Crepida sandal, lacing anchored a long tongue with animal head.

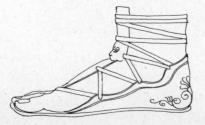

The toga is seen here folded longitudinally round the centre into thick folds and place over the left shoulder forming the hanging length down the front. The other part was passed obliquely over the back and under the right arm and then cast over the left shoulder, thus covering the left arm. The diagonal piece acted as a partial covering of the right arm. The folds in front were often used as a pocket, which were known as 'sinus'.

The details of Roman dress is derived from statues. The main articles of clothing were: an under-tunic, 'tunica interior', often sleeveless; an over-tunic, or stola, fitted with sleeves and cut in a similar fashion to the tunica interior, often with a train; a cloak or palla; and a veil earlier known as a 'flammeum' later a 'ricinium'. The whole appearance was similar to the male toga.

The veil attached towards the back of the head, then draped over the shoulder and the back.

Hair tightly curled across the front half of the head, then combed back to fall in loose waves to the neck.

Hair parted in the centre with curls or ringlets falling from the temples to the shoulders.

Roman – Ladies headdress styles with tiaras.

From a centre parting the hair is lightly waved to the nape of the neck where it ends in a chignon.

Close-cut hairstyle.

Saxons (700–1066)

Male styles

The development of the male costume in the post-Roman period remained simple. A plain, wide, loose, linen garment for the wealthy, and wool for the lower classes, was cut to the middle of the thigh, or knee length, and put on over the head. These short, knee-length tunics were sometimes slit up the sides to the hips to allow movement of the legs, the front often being caught between the legs and held at the waist. The opening for the neck was either round or square, often with a short vertical slit in front. This, more often than not, was decorated with a band of embroidery in coloured silks. The sleeves were close fitting to the wrists, but were full with circular puckers around the forearm, allowing them to hang over the hands for warmth. Encircling the waist was usually a narrow cloth or leather girdle, the tunic being very loosely pouched and pulled over it. This girdle supported a pouch wallet, and for the nobility a dagger or a sword.

The nobility, on ceremonial occasions, wore a long, ankle-length garment of very simple design with decorated borders in rich embroidery at the hem and neck. Over these tunics were worn the super-tunic or *roc*, as it was known by its Saxon name, which was loose fitting reaching just below the knees, sometimes sleeveless, or with very full sleeves fitting closely at the wrist. The outer tunic was fitted on over the head through a wide neck aperture. At this period it was not uncommon to wear a linen shirt next to the body beneath the tunic.

In inclement weather a voluminous cloak or mantle was

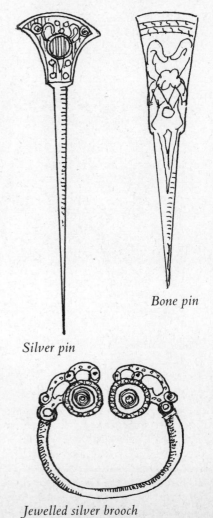

Bone pin

Silver pin

Jewelled silver brooch

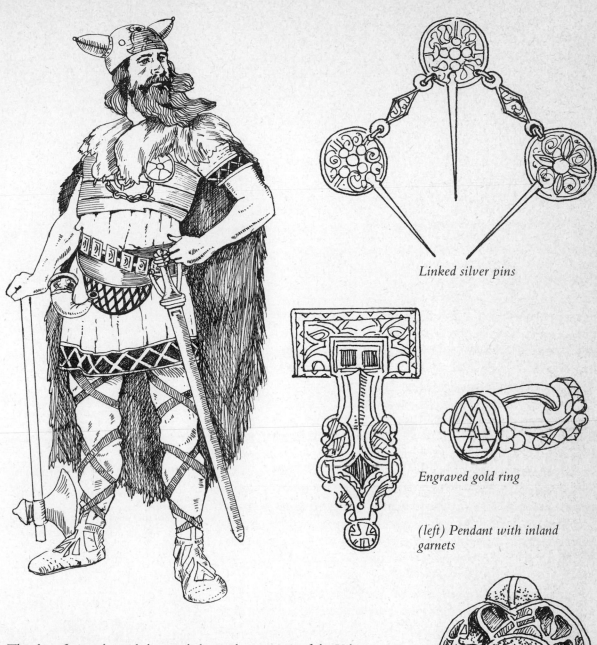

Linked silver pins

Engraved gold ring

(left) Pendant with inland garnets

Brooch

The close-fitting, horned, bronze helmet, characteristic of the Viking Anglo-Saxon period, was usually worn by chieftains, making them easily recognizable in battle. Over the embroidered tunic was worn a thick, leather corselet covered with metal scales. The loose, leg braies were bound with criss-cross leather gartering. The weapons carried were the bronze-hilted sword, which, like the blowing horn, was attached to a waisted belt made from metal pieces. A battle axe was carried and was a most formidable weapon of the period. Over the shoulders was flung a full mantle of fur.

worn, often embroidered, and fastened with a large clasp or brooch which was usually worn on the right shoulder or in front on the breast. The capes were square or rectangular in shape and varied from a short cape, *chape*, to a long, ankle-length mantle. Sometimes a *chasuble*, or large circular cloak with a hole in the centre for the head, was worn in varying lengths and was caught up at the sides and allowed to fall into a draped effect. For the higher ranks this was often lined in a contrasting colour. By the tenth century a large rectangular stole-shaped mantle was worn wrapped around the body from the waist, falling to the ground in loose folds, the free end being slung over the shoulder.

The legs were enclosed in loose breeches or *braies* which could be either long or short. When worn to the ankle, they were either tied at the ankle or bound with strips of cloth crosswise from the boot up to the thigh. This style was favoured by the nobility. Even with the short breeches the bare legs were bound with the same binding in a similar manner. These leg bandages sometimes replaced the use of stockings, being worn bound around the lower leg like puttees (narrow strips of cloth wound round the lower leg), with the free ends tucked in at the top, or more decoratively the ends were decorated with tassels and allowed to dangle. By the tenth century close-fitting short breeches and woollen tights had become popular.

Clothes made from skin and leather were often worn outdoors by working men, and indoors a woollen shirt or tunic to mid-thigh was worn over long, thick trousers which were fairly full-cut and cross-gartered. Leather belts had buckles similar to shoe buckles. The most popular leather was cow-hide, usually black for shoes.

FOOTWEAR

Shoes of leather, canvas and felt worn by both men and women were low cut, and sometimes the cross-gartering started from the tops. The Roman use of the iron last continued and the soles were made of leather. Also popular were soles made of plaited straw or wood. Shoe-making was a highly skilled craft. The basic shape of the shoe was plain, but decoration was used in the form of different coloured inlays under the intricate cut-out vamps, embroidery, jewels and appliqué patterns. Shoes or sandals in various forms were the accepted footwear throughout this period. They were, in general, simple and low, the higher raised heel being un-

(c.1025). Popular style of cloak fastening with a brooch on the right shoulder, complete with hood.

Popular pull-on style of the period, often plain.

16

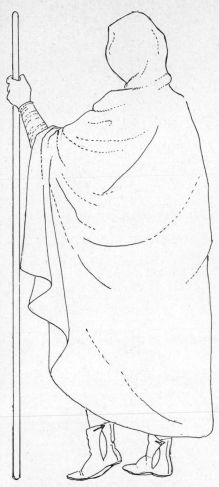

Back view showing the protective cloak.

known at this time. Some were close fitting round the ankle with either a central slit down the top of the shoe, or side slits with a central flap. Others were open around the ankle. They were fastened by leather thonging attached from behind, bound round the ankle and tied over the instep, while others had no fastening whatsoever. Soft mid-calf or shorter length boots were not uncommon; these often being laced up at the front. Open-topped sandal slippers with low vamps were also worn.

HEAD–WEAR

Head-wear was not as commonplace as in later periods, it was the fashion to go bareheaded. The usual head-gear, if worn, was the Phrygian bonnet, a small, close-fitting woollen cap with a pointed crown which hung forward. This was worn in various shapes and with decorations from the ninth to the end of the twelfth century. This type of hat was later chosen by the French Revolutionaries of 1793 as their 'Liberty Cap'.

Men's hair of the period was well combed and trimmed square across the neck, being well brushed back from the forehead and temples. The Saxon-type beard was often forked into two points, which was known as a *bifid* beard, and the wearing of moustaches was usual. Hair was worn fairly short in the ninth and tenth centuries. It was usually combed from the crown. Beards were only worn by the upper classes. In the early eleventh century the clergy encouraged the decline of beards, although beards and longer hair became fashionable again later, the hair being curled and plaited.

Plain, buttoned shoe with unstitched buttonholes, round-toed and high to the ankle.

The longer toed type of shoe, usually coloured, the collar matching the buttons.

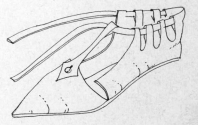

Pointed toe with two kinds of fastening: thonging through the loops round the ankle and a button on the vamp from the T-piece.

ACCESSORIES

Pouch wallets were carried either slung from the shoulder or from the girdle belt. Shoulder belts slung from the right shoulder over to the left side supported a sword, these being carried by the nobility only.

The wearing of gloves, although a Continental fashion, was adopted by the upper class and certain high ranking clergy. Bracelets of gold and bronze were worn around the arm. Materials used were rough wool and linen for the lower class and finer grades for the upper class. Furs were very fashionable with ermine and grey squirrel for the nobility, fox, otter, musk-rat and marten for the middle class and sheep and rabbit skins for the lower class. The predominating colours were brown, blue, red, green and yellow. Gold and silver thread and precious stones were used in embroidery decoration.

Early British hairstyle with long hair, beard and moustache.

Female styles

Like the male attire, the costume of the women in the post-Roman period developed on very simple lines. The *kirtle* or tunic, put on over the head, was worn over a chemise shirt garment. The tunic fell to the ground and was close fitting with a V-shaped neck opening, though more usually it was cut to a round form. The sleeves were long and tighter fitting, ending in a small cuff. The materials used were either linen or wool, the linen being for the upper class and the coarsely woven wool for the lower class.

Worn over the tunic was the super-tunic or roc. This garment, like the kirtle, was put on over the head. It was wide, falling in loose folds to the ground, and was usually hitched up over the girdle, waist belt, revealing the under-tunic to knee level. The sleeves were either cylindrical and loose, or wide becoming bell-shaped from just below the elbow. The girdle was usually wider than that worn by the men, and was the same colour as the super-tunic. For decoration the roc was embroidered around the neckline, sleeve-cuffs and hem.

English women were renowned for their needlework, and often the hems, sleeves and neck edges as well as panels down the front of tunics were lavishly embroidered in coloured thread, as well as in gold and silver.

The mantle, cut square, was either knee-length or full to the ground. This was usually hitched up in front, and

Cloak fastening on both shoulders, leaving the arms free (c.1040).

Anglo-Saxon with a large wrap-around cloak (c.1030).

Tenth-century style, page-boy type.

fastened under the chin by a brooch or a tie. The closed mantle was fashioned like the tunic, in as much as it was put on over the head and worn without a fastening. Sometimes called the double mantle, the closed mantle was lined with a material of contrasting colour.

Stockings were worn by the wealthier class, but were never exposed. Footwear came in various forms, following very closely the men's styles.

HEAD-WEAR

The outstanding feature of this period was the female head-wear. This consisted of a veil, or, as the Saxons called it, a *head-rail*. This was worn by all classes, not only in public, but also in their homes. A long, wide stole covered the head from the forehead and draped down at the back to the shoulders. Completely hiding the hair, it was set close to the face, leaving only the face visible. The ends of the stole were then passed over the shoulders in front and crossed over the bosom and allowed to fall to the knees. It was then draped in diverse ways according to the taste of the wearer. The head-rail was made in colours either matching or in contrast with the super-tunic. Although the hair was concealed, it was usually formed into plaits and such accessories as gold hair-ties and crispin needles (used to curl and plait hair) were used.

In the Saxon period no woman revealed her hair, which was covered by a head-rail or 'haefods-ragel'. During the Norman period this head-rail or *couvrechief*, as it was now known, became smaller.

Throughout the Anglo-Saxon period only single girls wore their hair loose. All other women wore their hair under a head-rail or veil. Under this the hair was worn either loose or plaited and was held in place with pins with ornamental heads, which also held the veils in place.

ACCESSORIES

Jewellery was very fashionable in the form of circlets of gold, neckbands, bracelets, rings, beads, ear-rings and jewelled girdles.

19

Normans (1066–1154)

Male styles

In the eleventh century the upper class wore simple garments, not so markedly different from the ordinary people. The distinction lay mainly in the richer, coloured fabrics and embroidered decorations. While wool and homespun linen were extensively used, silk was also used by the ruling classes. Men wore short under-garments which were made up of two tubes put on separately and which covered the lower section of the trunk, often reaching to the knee.

After the Norman conquest of Britain, the main difference in fashion between the conquerors and the vanquished was more in the manner of hairstyle than that of costume which showed remarkable similarity. The reason for this was the great intercourse of fashion between France and Britain which had taken place over many years prior to the invasion.

The tunic was now slightly closer fitting to the body, with the skirt becoming a little fuller. The method of putting on over the head remained the same. The neckline was either a moderately low, round aperture or a short, vertical slit down the front and secured with a brooch. As of previous times the tunic was short, being either knee or calf-length. The long, ankle-length tunic was worn only by the nobility on ceremonial occasions. As in the earlier fashion the tunic was often slit up on either side.

The skirt worn by the Normans was divided, cut and joined between the legs forming 'shorts'.

The sleeves changed only slightly, the upper part being puckered and full, narrowing from the elbow and fitting

A Norman fashion of a divided skirt or 'shorts'.

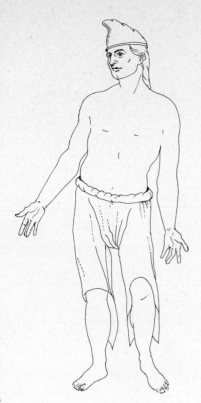

Braies secured by a running string at the waist.

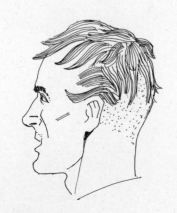

Norman style, hair shaven at back level to the ears, the rest cut short and brushed forward, usually clean shaven.

close to the wrist, or cut short, hanging wide from the elbow.

Girdles of cloth or leather were worn but were usually concealed by hitching up and pouching the tunic to overhang. Embroidered woven bands decorated the tunics round the neck, upper arms, wrists and hem.

The *super-tunic*, which was worn over the tunic, remained a loose garment, often made in a circular form and put on over the head. It was made to fit over the tunic, a little shorter in length, to expose the embroidered hem of the tunic. Sleeves could be loose and wide, becoming bell-shaped at the wrist, then turned back to become a wide broad cuff. Sometimes the sleeves were close fitting.

Girdles were occasionally worn and used to hitch up and shorten the length of the super-tunic.

Breeches, or braies, which were loose fitting, covered the legs from the waist downwards, sometimes with foot pieces attached or with loops of material under the foot. They were supported by a running cord through the waistline of the breeches. The wealthier class wore the breeches fitting close to the leg from the knee to the ankle. Leg bandages, which were strips of either linen or wool, were wrapped spirally, or for the nobility in a criss-cross pattern, from the ankle to just below the knee. Both breeches and stockings were cut on the cross.

Coarse stockings were worn, these being made of wool or linen and shaped to the leg (knitting was still unknown in England). They were always knee-length, ending in an embroidered border just below the knee.

The leather shoes were pointed and shaped to the feet. They were heel-less, high over the instep and fitted close to the ankle with a short tongue, or were slit down the instep and fastened with thongs.

The continuing fashion of going bare-headed remained. For bad weather the *cowl* or hood which was attached to the cloak, or alternatively the Saxon Phrygian cap, was worn.

Norman men shaved their hair level with the ears with the rest of the hair brushed down the front. Occasionally they had long moustaches, but more usually they were clean-shaven. This Norman fashion soon lost its popularity, and the Normans began to follow the British by wearing long, flowing hair, a style which was to last until the end of the eleventh century. The hair was parted in the centre with either a fringe or brushed back. Moustaches and beards were worn mainly by the older men, the beards often being forked.

Female styles

The *gunna* or kirtle was similar to the male tunic, but was long and fell in folds to the ground. This was worn over the chemise or smock which was worn next to the skin. Women at this time did not wear underwear such as braies or drawers. A girdle was always worn. The sleeves were long, close-fitting and tight at the wrist. Over the kirtle was worn the super-tunic or *roc*, which was long and loose, covering the kirtle completely. The sleeves were loose and flowing, opening to a bell shape at the wrist. Occasionally a slightly closer-fitting sleeve was worn. Sleeves were often tubular in shape and came well over the hand being used as gloves or a muff.

The mantle, although similar in cut to the masculine cloak, was generally closed and put on over the head. It was of ground length. Unlike the male mantle, the mantle of the female was not hooded.

Stockings made of cloth were cut similarly to the men's, often reaching above the knees and fastened by ties. Footwear followed the fashionable male styles.

The veil at first was a circle with a hole cut in the centre, the remainder being draped over the shoulders and head. Later, the veil became oblong in shape with a semi-circular shape cut out to frame the face, allowing the rest of the lightweight material to hang in folds. In winter a longer rectangular veil was draped around the neck and under the chin. This method was also practical for fastening at the sides so that while working, the veil would not hang in the way.

Circlets of gold or material which could be embroidered were worn either over or under the veils.

The hair remained concealed beneath the Saxon head-rail, now called a *coverchief* (the French, *couvre-chef*), kerchief or a veil, which was smaller than the original and earlier head-rail and was either rectangular in shape or slightly circular. The straight edge lay forward from the forehead, which covered the hair, then hung in folds around the face, neck and tops of the shoulders. It was crossed over in front and often wound round like a scarf. Young girls were allowed to wear their hair long and flowing. All accessories were similar to those of the previous century.

Long hair worn with a centre parting with moustache and forked beard (c.1090).

The close-fitting gown from shoulder to hip level fastened at the back. The skirt hung in heavy folds to the ground with the sleeves close fitting to the wrist. A long girdle was worn at hip level. A long veil covered the head and was kept in place by a circlet (c.1070).

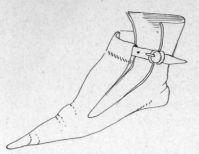

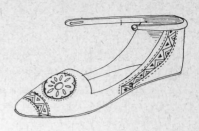

High backed with buckle fastening.

Slipper type buttoned at the ankle.

Ankle boot, jewelled and decorated for the richer class.

(below right) The Norman soldier's armour, called 'hauberk', was made of chainmail, and knee length. It was slit front and back with wide sleeves reaching to the elbow. It had a rectangular patch on the chest. The helmet was conical with a nasal piece on the lower edge. The legs were covered with loose trousers or braies. The shield was kite shaped, made of wood and covered with leather (c.1066).

A bell-shaped super-tunic worn over the close-fitting tight-sleeved tunic. A veil covered the head and draped round the shoulders and neck (c.1135).

(above) The short-sleeved tunic was fairly loose fitting to the knees, and put on over the head. The neckline, being low cut, revealed the under-tunic with the close-fitting sleeves and neckline. The braies covered the legs from the waist with crossbands from the knee to the ankle. The shoes were of leather (c.1080).

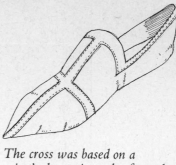

The cross was based on a priest's decoration, also formed design for armour.

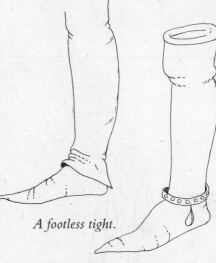

Close-fitting gown with extremely wide sleeves and full-length cloak. The hair in two plaits hung down to the knees and was bound with ribbon. A long veil was worn with a circlet of gold and precious stones (1125–1175).

A footless tight.

Boot above knee length with top of contrasting colour.

Fishtail shoe, known as 'pigases', with padded toes.

Scorpian shoe with turned-up and stuffed point.

(left) Two tunics worn, one over the other, the outer- or super-tunic had wide sleeves with the emphasis on the cuffs, and laced up at the back. Back view of the long super-tunic showing the back-lacing (1100–1120).

TOP: *Roman legionnaire in marching order (c.400).*

LEFT: *Anglo-Saxon with simple loose-fitting tunic reaching the knees.*
Cloak fastened with brooch at the shoulder (c.1060).
RIGHT: *Norman wearing a long under-tunic with an embroidered*
outer-tunic and wide sleeves (c.1087).

Norman lady with a close-fitting bodice and full skirt with exaggerated sleeves (c. 1136).

LEFT: *Norman lady wearing under- and over-tunic, similar to the male fashion (c. 1130).*

RIGHT: *Short-haired man in Norman fashion with short tunic and a divided skirt or 'shorts' (c. 1100).*

Flat, wide-brimmed hat worn over a hood (c.1154).

The Plantagenets (1154–1399)

Male styles

Styles of clothes for both male and female changed little during the Plantagenet period (1154–1399). The style and quality depended mainly on the rank of the wearer.

TUNIC

Close-fitting bodices worn during the reign of Stephen (1135–1154) were no longer in fashion by the beginning of Henry II's reign (1154–1189). The sleeves became tight-fitting at the wrists, but wide at the armholes. Although basically fashionable costume remained very much as it was in the previous century, variations began to appear with both long and short tunics. The tunic was cut with a closer fit to the body and the longer skirt was slit up the front to thigh level, the tunic being worn with or without a girdle. The girdle, when worn, had one hanging end.

The sleeves were wide and loose from the armhole opening and were close fitting with the bell-shaped type of cuff at the wrist. Sometimes the sleeve extended to form a large cuff which could be rolled back to bare the arm. A very close, tight-fitting, embroidered, turned-back cuff was not uncommon. Worsted cloth of scarlet wool was much favoured by the nobility.

The super-tunic or over-tunic remained unchanged and was now often worn alone, and never with the close-fitting tunic. When lined with fur, the super-tunic was called a *pelisson*.

High crowned hat with wide turned-up brim worn over a hood (1154–1199).

CLOAK

Cloaks and mantles remained full and wide, being fastened with an ornamental clasp, brooch or cord. Not uncommon

Small, round stalked hat worn over a white linen coif and tied under the chin (1199–1216).

was the method of fastening by pulling one side through a ring which was sewn in one corner, then tied into a knot to hold it in position. For travellers and country people, the cloaks were sometimes made of skins with hoods attached, the hair side of the skin being on the outside.

Breeches and braies became shorter, to knee length, and formed drawers, later to be used as under-garments.

FOOTWEAR

Long hose were worn, some with and some without feet, while others had a stirrup strap which passed under the foot. Those with fitted feet sometimes had thin leather soles and were worn without shoes – an earlier Saxon fashion which became popular again in the 1160s. They were made from either wool or thin leather. Bright colours and vertical stripes also became fashionable.

Stockings were either short, ending just below the knee with ornamental garter borders, or were long to about mid-thigh, close fitting to the leg and becoming slightly bell-shaped above the knee so that they could be pulled over the shortened braies. They finished with a protruding piece in front which was attached by a tie to the breeches girdle.

Low-cut shoes were very popular with the wealthier classes, while the poorer people retained the ankle-hugging kind. The calf-length variety with the turned-down uppers, which revealed the coloured linings, were gaining in popularity. Although many shoes followed the earlier patterns, they were becoming more pointed. Shoes were made from various materials such as cow-hide, fish-skins and cloth.

To be fashionable, shoes and small boots were laced on the inner side, the ladies' shoes not being quite as pointed as the men's. Shoes were mostly made to fit either foot and called *straights*. With wear they became a pair, the feet shaping them through use. The points which had become short, now became slightly longer and were stuffed with hair or wool. These were known as *pigaces*. This long, pointed shoe style was adopted from the Orient, possibly introduced by the Crusaders.

HEAD-WEAR

Head-wear was now gradually changing, the Phrygian cap, which had been popular since the tenth century, was by the twelfth century worn less and eventually became un-fashionable. A separate hood had become the most popular

A short, pointed hood with gorget, short tunic and the loose braies worn by the middle class (1130–1150).

Hose fitting the leg fastened to the belt of the breeches (c.1155).

Tunic and super-tunic with an ornate girdle. A small, round cap and low-cut shoes were also worn (c.1150).

Small beret type hat worn by the upper classes (c.1189).

head-covering. The hood had a loose, pointed cowl with a short cape attached, which covered the shoulders. Soft, stalked caps, not unlike the modern French beret, were also popular. Small, round caps with a stalk, or sometimes with a narrow rolled brim, were very fashionable.

Low-crowned hats with large brims were frequently worn over the hood. Small, round-crowned hats with a turned-down brim, decorated with a small, centrally placed knob were also worn. A close-fitting linen bonnet, called a *coif*, which covered both the hair and ears, was becoming very popular. The side strings were passed under the chin and tied. The coif could be worn alone or under other types of head-wear.

HAIR STYLES

Long hair to the shoulders and beards with moustaches were now back in favour. The hair could be parted on either side, the front hair being combed forward in a fringe over the forehead. During this period the moustache was never worn without a beard. However, most of the younger men preferred to be clean shaven with the hair cut short to the nape of the neck. Beards became forked and were sometimes covered in ointments and covered with special bags at night. It was fashionable for the hair to have two partings, bringing part of the hair forward on to the forehead and allowing the rest to hang down in curls and waves.

In King Stephen's reign (1135–1154) hair, although still long, was slightly shorter, and the hair that was brought forward from the double parting, was now only a simple lock on the forehead reaching the eyebrows. The long beards and the moustaches of the older men were waved and curled.

ACCESSORIES

Girdles were now highly decorated and tied like a sash with a purse often attached to one of the hanging ends; other girdles retained the ornamental buckle fastening. Small and large pouches were carried either from the girdle outside, or hidden under the tunic and slung from the breeches girdle (*braier*) along with the keys.

Gloves, heavily embroidered and inlaid with jewels, were worn only by the nobility.

Dagging, a form of vandyking (material which has notched or indented edges) began to appear round the bottom edge of the tunic or super-tunic, these being cut with deep indentations.

27

Female styles

The kirtle or gown style continued to be worn over the chemise or smock, similar to that of the male tunic. The gradual change of costume began to appear in the first quarter of the twelfth century. It was not a great upheaval of fashion, and was mainly confined to the ladies of the nobility.

The bodice was cut to fit the body more closely to hip level; the skirt was now cut considerably fuller and fell to the ground in loose folds, sometimes forming a train behind. Because of the tightness of the bodice, it was impossible to put the garment on over the head. Possibly it was fastened by being laced either in the front or at the back. The neck-line was either round without a *décolletage* or cut with a V-shape in front, sometimes deep enough to reveal the top of the chemise. The sleeves were close-fitting from the upper arm to just below the elbow, opening into bell shapes with long, hanging cuffs, often reaching the ground. Sometimes the long skirts and hanging cuffs were tied into knots, both as a fashionable trend, and also to keep them out of the way.

By 1130 clothes were more shaped to the body. The neck of the gown was cut low to reveal the chemise, and occasionally the super-tunic was omitted.

A girdle was always worn; it was fastened round the hips and then tied in front with the ends hanging down the centre, almost to the ground. Sometimes it was fastened at the back with the ends brought forward.

The cloak remained similar to the earlier style, the hooded variety becoming popular towards the end of the century.

HAIR STYLES

During the first half of the twelfth century, hair was allowed to be visible. It was worn with a centre parting with plaits either side, or was bound and interwoven with ribbons, to give a cross-gartered effect. The hair was worn long and could be made to look fuller by the addition of false hair. Length was also achieved by attaching metal cylinders to the ends of the plaits or encasing the hair in silk with ornamental tassels at the ends to hold the hair down.

In about 1120 plaits were divided into four, two hanging at the back, and two over the shoulders in the front. Plaits were worn until about 1170 when they became shorter and were worn crossed at the back and brought forward and secured above the forehead, similar to the Grecian styles.

At the beginning of the Plantagenet period, in the middle

(left) The low, round-necked gown fastened at the back had exaggerated turned-back sleeves; the skirt hung in heavy folds to the ground (1154–89).

(below) The two tunics worn over one another became one in a seamed gown with finely pleated skirt and long, hanging sleeves. A long girdle was worn. A crespine was worn over the head (c. 1199)

(left) The long gown was a close to the body-fitting fashion. The sleeves became a characteristic and exaggerated part of the style. The wide cuff became an extreme streamer which was knotted to prevent it from trailing the ground and was known as a 'tippet'. The hair was worn long, parted in the centre and allowed to fall to waist length in two plaits bound by ribbons (1199–1216).

of the twelfth century, long plaits became less popular, and the hair was again hidden, but by a much smaller veil. The plaits were worn either coiled over the ears or at the back of the head, and were covered with a shorter couvrechef.

HEAD-WEAR

Two styles of headdress, the *barbette* and *wimple*, became popular, but the covered-up appearance did not last long, and it became fashionable to have more hair visible. The barbette, probably introduced by Henry II's wife, Eleanor of Aquitaine, was a linen band around the head, encircling the face and fastened on the top, worn with a smaller veil and crown.

The head-wear or coifs adorned not only the head, but the face as well. The open veil was always worn by noble ladies in public, especially during the first half of the century. Head-bands were worn over the veil to keep it in place, these being placed round the head over the veil and fastened on one side, the long ends hanging down in a flowing style.

The head-gear was basically a little cap, black or white, which fitted on to the head, over which was worn the various styles of feminine head attire. The French fashion of linen head-band, or fillet, worn with the linen band, or barbette, which was worn under the chin to the temples and fastened at the side of the head. Fashionable also was the wimple or *gorget* head-wear. This consisted of a long, white linen or silk front-neck covering, draped over the bosom. The ends were caught up and swathed around the chin, framing the face, and then pinned to the hair above the ears, or under the veil on top of the head.

The hair was usually concealed under the veil. Young girls wore their hair uncovered, with a centre parting, the hair falling to the shoulders. Hair worn parted in the centre and then plaited into long tresses which hung down over the shoulders in front, almost to the knees, was a new style, introduced by the nobility. Hair was often bedecked with ornamentation of false hair, ribbons or encased in silk tubes called *fouriaux*. This new style was worn with a veil and head-band or circlets of gold or stylized diadems. Sometimes the hair was gathered into gold nets called *crespines*.

ACCESSORIES

Jewellery of bracelets, rings, necklaces and brooches were worn. Gloves, although rare at this period, were worn only by the nobility. Face make-up of rouge was generally used by the upper classes.

The Thirteenth Century

Male styles

The earlier modes remained fashionable but newer cuts in style appeared, these being typical of the thirteenth century.

TUNIC

The *cote* or tunic was now fitted with the sleeves made in one piece with the bodice. The sleeve had a wide armhole from the shoulder to the waist, being shaped and cut to slope to a very narrow, close-fitting cuff at the wrist. All tunics were slit up the front to the waist.

The super-tunic, now called a *surcote*, continued to be worn in the old style by the unfashionable, although the girdle was worn less.

The *tabard* style, which first appeared at this time, was without sleeves with a front and back reaching to lower calf-level. The neck aperture was large enough to allow the head through. The front and back were joined together at waist level, either by clasps, or sewn together. The centre front was slit from the waist down. A girdle was never worn with a tabard.

The *garde-corps* or *herygoud* (or herygaud), was a wide, loose voluminous surcote, which fell in loose folds down to the ankles, or just below knee level. The sleeves were wide and tubular in shape, the fullness being gathered in at the shoulders and falling well below hand-length. In the front of the upper arm of the sleeve was a vertical slit through which the arm could be passed. The herygoud was usually fitted with a hood. Generally no girdle was worn.

Sleeveless type of super-tunic worn open at the sides over the tunic and fastened with a belt (c.1236).

30

Super-tunic hanging down loose to the calf with hood attached. Small beret worn over a coif (c.1272).

A surcote with short wide sleeves which fell loosely to just below elbow length was often worn. Sometimes a girdle was worn with this style.

The *garnache* variety of surcote was similar in style to the tabard, the shoulder line cut large for the cloth to droop down to the elbows on either side, making a caped-sleeve effect. This was worn without a girdle. The sides of the garnache, similar to the tabard, were either joined by a clasp just below waist level, sewn from the waist to the hem, or left open down the sides.

In the middle of the century, pockets, or *fitchets* began to make their appearance. These were at first just vertical slit-openings in the surcote. Through these slits the wallet or keys, which were attached to the girdle of the surcote, could be reached.

Cloaks and leg-wear remained unchanged generally. The criss-cross strip-cloth bandaging around the legs became unfashionable for the nobility.

Foot-wear changed very little. Shoes, shaped to the feet, were plain and close to the ankle with lacing or buckle fastenings, or open and cut high behind the ankles with ankle or instep straps. *Buskins*, or boots, which were loose fitting, reached to just below the calf.

HEAD-WEAR AND HAIR STYLE

The coif seemed to be the most popular form of head-wear, although a hood, sometimes without a gorget (cape), was much in evidence. Stalked, round hats, large-brimmed travelling hats and broad-brimmed hats, worn cocked either at the front or back, and bowler-type round-crown hats continued to be worn.

The hair was bobbed with a centre parting and worn either with a straight or waved fringe. Beards and moustaches were cut much shorter than in the previous period. In the thirteenth century, short, fluffy hair, still being curled with crisping irons, became fashionable, with beards and moustaches becoming shorter. Centre partings and fringes were also popular for a short time.

In King John's reign (1199–1216) men's hair became shoulder length with a short fringe and the sides were brushed into loose waves and rolled at the ends.

A coif, a white linen cap, was often worn and remained popular throughout the Middle Ages.

In the first quarter of the thirteenth century the majority

Peasant farm-hand with hitched-up tunic (c. 1270)

of men had their hair parted at the top just above the fore-head, the fringe was curled, the sides were loosely waved and the ends curled over.

The younger men still preferred to be clean-shaven.

ACCESSORIES
The wearing of accessories did not change during this period to any marked degree. Gloves continued to be worn only by the nobility, although towards the end of the century they had become a little more popular. Glove-makers were recorded as early as 1295.

Female styles

The gown, also known as a cote, remained very much in the style of the twelfth century, altering in the neckline shape only. It was becoming slightly lower with a V-shape opening fastened by a clasp or brooch. The fullness with the loose folds to the ground was retained; the waist was encircled with a girdle. The sleeves were either close-fitting or wide, both being fashionable.

About the middle of the thirteenth century the cote was fitted with pockets, or fitchets similar to those found in the male surcote. Through these fitchets the purse or keys, which were suspended from the smock or chemise girdle, could be reached.

The surcote, which was put on over the head through a wide neck aperture, was long to the ground, wide and voluminous with loose folds. Until mid-century the sleeves were wide, reaching to the middle of the lower arm. After this date, they become closer fitting. Like the male garment, they were worn without a girdle.

A sleeveless surcote was also worn. Although similar in style, the neck aperture was wide, giving a large shoulder-strap effect. The armholes were just long vertical slits at the side. Like the sleeved surcote, it was worn without a girdle. The fur-lined surcote, or pelisson made from squirrel, fox or rabbit, continued to be worn.

CLOAKS
Cloaks and mantles similar to the twelfth-century style continued to be worn. They were long to the ground, had a train and occasionally were hooded for travelling. Mantles were now also being used as dressing-gowns, often made of

Lady in long cloak drawn up and carried over the arm (c. 1270)

Barbette and wimple worn beneath a crown (c. 1270).

The open-sided super-tunic. The skirt was draped into the side opening while working, the hem of the gown being turned up and pinned, revealing the underskirt. The hair was pulled back into side coils and covered with a linen cap (1216–1272).

The linen fillet worn around the head with a barbette, the hair hidden under a crespine (c.1250).

silk and occasionally lined with fur. Hoods were worn mainly by the middle and lower-classes when any head protection was required. They were similar to those worn by men. During the reign of Edward I (1272–1307), the hoods had a long tubular protrusion called a *liripipe*, which was often very long.

Leg-wear, such as stockings and shoes, followed the men's style of the previous century.

HEAD-WEAR AND HAIR STYLE

The barbette, fillet, wimple and veil remained as before, only the shape of the fillet changing to suit the change of coiffure. Generally the hair was taken up at the neck and pinned to the barbette which was draped under the chin and pinned to the top of the head. The hair was sometimes contained in a net, or fret, which was never worn by itself except by the lower classes.

The *wimple*, also worn with a veil, was adopted in about 1190 and remained in fashion for about 200 years. This consisted of a length of fine material wound just under the chin, and the ends pinned to the hair each side, or to the crown of the head.

The *fillet*, often pleated or goffered, was a stiffened linen or silk band worn round the head and over the barbette. This became fashionable during the reign of Henry III (1216–1272). It varied in width from about 3 cm to 10 cm. The hair was left flowing for young girls, but it was more usual for the hair to be worn coiled at the nape of the neck.

A net or *caul*, known as a crespine, was worn with the fillet or barbette, and this was popular for a long time. The crespine was attached to a band worn round the head.

From the end of the thirteenth century to the reign of Edward II (1307–1327), it was fashionable for hair to be worn in coiled plaits over the ears. The crespine, still worn in its original form, was adapted to cover the coils by being divided, the two parts being joined by a head-band.

The hair, although seldom revealed, was brushed back from the forehead where it could be plaited and coiled into a roll at the back of the head and covered with a net.

After the middle of the century the hair was often parted in the centre and the side hair plaited and coiled on each side over the ears, then covered with a net. Wide, goffered fillets were usually fitted. Flowers in garlands or chaplets (crants, craunce or craundice) made from gold, iron, or linen decorated with real or artificial flowers ornamented the hair of the young girls.

The *ram's horn* style with the hair parted in the centre, the plaits twisted over each ear and the ends pulled out to form the 'horn', was popular towards the end of the thirteenth century. During the first half of the fourteenth century this style was worn with a wimple draped and pinned over these plaits, and was tucked into the neck of the bodice and became known as the gorget. The plaits were also wrapped round the head from ear to ear, with small curls hanging over the gorget. A decorative metal fillet, and occasionally a veil, was worn with this style. Jewellery continued to be worn by the nobility, rings, necklaces, bracelets as well as gloves and other accessories.

A band pleated on to a stiffened piece of linen covering the crown of the head (1250–1300).

A metal-worker with protective leather apron.

The hair covered with a fret or caul (c.1300).

Early Fourteenth Century

Short tunic with loose, hanging sleeves. Liripipe hood and gorget also worn (c.1307).

Short cote-hardie with long streamers or tippets hanging from the elbow. A dagged-edged hood and cape were worn over this. Parti-coloured hose were also fashionable (c.1366).

Male styles

The later styles of the thirteenth century continued in fashion until the first half of the fourteenth century. These styles then gradually became unfashionable with a noticeable trend to the closer fitting, more shapely and better-cut clothes. The move was towards shorter styles, which revealed leg-wear. The tunic, as such, was now mainly worn by the lower class. It had wide sleeves and was worn with a girdle.

DOUBLET

Replacing the tunic in the fashionable upper class was the *doublet*, known as a *gipon* or *pourpoint* by about 1335. This was worn over the shirt and had a close-fitting padded and waisted bodice, falling straight, without folds to just above the knee, and fastened from neck to hem either by lacing or a close row of buttons. The neckline was round and low cut. The sleeves, which were close fitting and tight to the wrist, were fastened with a row of buttons from wrist to elbow. The girdle was seldom worn at first, and was worn only and always with the *cote-hardie*, but later, when the cote-hardie was discarded, a girdle was worn with the gipon.

OUTER-GARMENTS

The cote-hardie, which had earlier replaced the super-tunic, was worn as an over-garment by the upper class, and covered the gipon. It was close-fitting with a low neckline, and was fastened down the front to the waist either by lacing or by buttons. The skirt section was full with a centre opening falling to knee level. The sleeves finished at the elbow, and draped at the back into a short hanging flap. This varied both in length and width to suit individual tastes. The belt, when worn, was usually positioned below waist level.

The cote-hardie when worn by the lower classes was wider and looser, often without a front fastening. The neckline was large, enabling the garment to be put on over the head. It was folded over in front, closing the neckline, and was fastened by pinning. The skirt part was either knee or ankle-length, being open at the front to the girdle. The sleeves followed the fashionable trend of the period. A girdle was worn either at waist level or just below. When the girdle was not worn, fitchets were often in evidence.

The garnache altered little during this period. The only noticeable change was in the collar, which now had two small tongue-shaped lapels of a different shade of material, or was fur-trimmed at the neck.

The garde-corps and the tabard styles were now becoming unfashionable although the super-tunic and the mantles continued to be worn. Long, circular-cut cloaks fastened in front or buttoned on the right shoulder were worn, often with expensive and lavish linings for the nobility.

Shoulder capes without hoods were popular and remained so for a long period. Low-collared capes which were cut circular and fell to just below the knee were very common. These fastened by a close row of buttons down the front and sometimes hoods were attached.

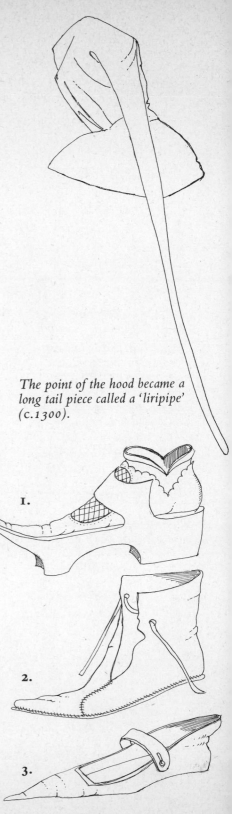

The point of the hood became a long tail piece called a 'liripipe' (c.1300).

1.

2.

3.

FOOTWEAR

Stockings continued to be worn in varying lengths: either knee or thigh-length or socks which reached to just below the calf. The soled hose, with a thin leather sole attached, were worn without footwear and continued to be worn until the end of the fifteenth century. The hose were often decorated in contrasting colours, for example one leg could even be divided in vertical stripes in different colours. Long stockings were attached with buttons to the thigh which had a string hanging from the braie girdle. Garters, which were strips of linen, were tied just below the knee, the strip ends either left hanging or tucked in.

Well-cut shoes, which were shaped to the foot and pointed at the big toe, were worn. These fitted round the ankle, lacing at either side, or sometimes with a flap across the long tongue. Some were shaped slipper-fashion, being cut away

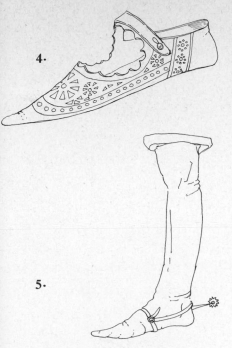

4.

5.

1 *A patten cut from one piece of wood, worn over a decorated shoe.*

2 *Thick, leather shoe with sole attached with thread.*

3 *Soft, open shoe with strap.*

4 *Embroidered, soft shoe with leather sole, rose-window style.*

5 *Fashionably shaped riding boot with spur attached with leather strap.*

Eccentric hood fashion. The face opening was put over the head and the edge rolled back to form a brim. The gorget hung down one side. (c. 1320)

over the instep and attached and fastened round the ankle with a strap and buckle.

For the upper classes, shoes were decorated by embroidery or by patterns punched into the leather. Riding boots were shaped to the thighs and fastened with buttons, lace or buckles just below the calf. Other styles were loose and shapeless, being pulled round to fit the leg with a fold in front and then fastened down the outside of the calf by either buttons or hooks.

The wearing of spurs, which were strapped to the ankles over the soled hose, was very fashionable, even for civilians. From about 1300 spurs became fitted with *rowls* (spiked wheels) in place of the simple spike.

HEAD–WEAR AND HAIR STYLES

Remaining in fashion was the hood which had now developed an extension of a hanging tail-piece from the point of the cowl, which was called a liripipe. This appendage could be long or short, and was made in one piece with the hood. If cut vertically, the liripipe would hang down either side, but if it were cut horizontally, it would hang down the centre back. The liripipe could be styled by twisting it around the head in a turban fashion.

The stalked beret of the thirteenth century continued in fashion, especially for the country people. Also popular was the small crowned hat with a wide brim, which was turned up at the back and brought to a long peak in front, and the high, bowler-shaped crown with a narrow, turned-up brim. The turban-fashioned head-wear, which was created from the hood, became known as the *hood turban* later in the century. The coif, too, was still very popular.

Hair styles still maintained the thirteenth-century look with the clean-shaven face. Beards both with and without moustaches were popular and were common, but side whiskers were not often seen. Extremely fashionable was the rolled curl over the forehead and at the nape of the neck, worn with a clean-shaven face.

ACCESSORIES

The girdle was now very ornamental, tied in front with the long ends dangling down the centre front. A pouch or purse was carried, slung by two straps from the girdle, and was carried by all classes.

A dagger, worn mainly by the nobility, was carried hang-

Workmen building a house, early 14th century

ing vertically suspended from a cord tied to the girdle, or attached to the back of the pouch.

Gloves were now worn universally by all classes. They usually had a gauntlet cuff, which for the upper class was embroidered. The lower classes wore a type of mitten which was made with the thumb and first finger separate, while the other three fingers were made in one. The glove-makers of London were recognized as a separate organization in *c*.1349.

Female styles

KIRTLE

In the first quarter of the fourteenth century the women's kirtle or gown continued almost unaltered, but by about

A very high crowned, beaver hat decorated with a feather was very popular during this period (c.1350).

The hair was straight ending in a turned-up roll at ear level, the top hair being combed forward over the forehead in an uneven fringe (c.1340).

1330 a great fundamental change took place in the cote-hardie. It now showed the shape of the figure to the hips, where the skirt section widened suddenly and fell to the ground in expanding folds. The neckline was low cut, often revealing the shoulders. The sleeves were long and close fitting and were buttoned or sewn from the wrist to the elbow. The gown had either a front or a back fastening, by lacing from the neckline to the waist. A girdle, which was sometimes worn at hip level, could be seen through the side vents of the sleeveless over-garment.

OUTER–GARMENTS

The cote-hardie was similar in cut to the male garment. It was long, close fitting and waisted with a deep neckline, and was fastened down the front to just below the waist. With a wide neckline, it was put on over the head. The sleeves, of elbow length, widened into either small or large hanging flaps. The vertical fitchets or placket slits in the skirt were very popular.

Still in common use was the sleeved surcoat in its loose shapeless form; sometimes it had the side vents. The length varied from ground level to just below the knees. The sleeves were close fitting to the elbows, and widened below into a large cuff effect. The sleeveless surcoat also remained in common use, often with the side slits just above the hem. As with the sleeved surcoat, no girdle was worn.

Outer garments, in the form of hooded cloaks, were long to the ground and were worn especially for warmth and travelling. Lavishly lined mantles fastened with tasselled cords and jewelled ornamentation were worn on ceremonial occasions.

The garde-corps were now worn as outer wraps and the short pelissons were still very popular.

FOOTWEAR

Woollen or linen stockings remained unchanged, being held up by garters either above or below the knees. Women's footwear followed very closely that of male fashion, but was not as pointed.

HEAD–WEAR AND HAIR STYLES

Wimples and veils were still the fashionable head-gear and worn in the old style. Often the veil was worn alone by being placed over the head, then formed into a coif close to the shape of the head. It was then fastened down by a fillet placed low on the head and pinned into position, with the two end pieces allowed to fall down the back in a streamer fashion. Without the fillet, a fret or net was worn, which covered the hair completely with the exception of the side hair at the temple.

The barbette, now far more fashionable wear, was worn over the head outside of the net. The fillet had now become much narrower for popular wear. The fret was frequently very highly coloured with coloured spots. When the head-wear was worn without the barbette, and only the fret and the fillet worn, the fret was placed well down over the hair, the hair being formed into coils around the ears. The fillet was worn low on the head and came across the upper forehead.

Hoods were now commonplace for women of all classes, both for warmth and for travelling. Country women wore them on all occasions. The hoods were drawn over the face for funerals as an act of mourning. Hoods were open in front, the gorget being folded across the neck or fastened with buttons from the chin to the hem and, unlike the male hood, was not put on over the head, as it was worn over the female head-wear.

Although the hair was completely covered by either a fret or a veil, it was the fashion to wear the hair plaited and coiled round the ears on either side. Another hair fashion was to have vertical plaits set close to the face. The plaits were supported by the narrow fillet with stiff vertical strips.

ACCESSORIES

The fashion of wearing large aprons tied round the waist was more often confined to country women. These aprons were frequently embroidered. Gloves were now being worn by all classes following the male fashion. Jewellery also tended to follow male styles.

The wimple and veil style worn with a circlet (c.1305).

A veil worn over a wimple-type headdress (c. 1310).

A wimple worn without a veil, pinned over the coils of hair either side, and often known as a 'gorget'.

The wimple and veil worn with a goffered front piece (c.1325).

A street scene of the middle 14th century.

The Later Fourteenth Century

Male styles

DOUBLET

By the 1370s the gipon, now called a doublet for civilian use, continued to be fashionable. It was waisted and close fitting, being buttoned or laced down the front. The changes in fashion gave a padded front, which made a 'pigeon chest' appearance. The skirts of the gipon were becoming very much shorter, just covering the hips. Often these were buttoned up at the short side-vents. The sleeves were close fitting and buttoned from the elbow to the wrist. Sometimes this was sewn up. Among the new variations introduced were the long sleeves which came over the knuckles and then fanned out into a funnel shape. Worn, but rarely in England, was the *grande assiette*, a sleeve shape which was cut so that the sleeve had a circular seam which overlapped the front and back of the bodice section. The neckline was low and round until the 1420s, then followed the standing collar fashion.

Strings, or *estaches*, began to be sewn on the under side of the gipon for the attachment of the hose. Formerly these were suspended from the girdle of the drawers. The gipon, which was now worn without an over-garment, required a girdle.

OUTER-GARMENTS

The cote-hardie was now fastened in the centre front from neck to hem as opposed to the previous fastening to the waist only. The sleeves were close fitting to the elbow. The hanging

Short, high-necked houppelande with long, bagpipe-type sleeves, as well as long soled-hose were worn (c. 1399).

cuff was now longer and narrower, being a straight piece of material which hung down to just below the knees. A small upper band round the elbow formed a cuff effect. This was known as a 'tippet', but also had the French name of *coudière*. The length of the cote-hardie became very much shorter and was now often dagged. Towards the end of the century it had developed a collar. Long sleeves which were fastened with buttons down the forearm, developing into bell shapes over the hands, were popular. A highly ornamental girdle was worn round the hips and was fastened in front with long dangling ends in the centre.

From 1400 the centre buttoning of the cote-hardie became unfashionable and was replaced with hooks and eyes which were concealed by pleats. An extreme fashion which was worn by the dandies of the day, 'the Exquisites', was the very short cote-hardie which ended at the crotch.

Knights wore a broad girdle, often highly decorated with metal medallions joined together and fastened in front by a buckle. This was worn at hip level.

The garnache continued to be worn with a small change of design, a small tongue-shaped lapel at the neck.

The *houppelande* was introduced towards the end of the century (about 1380) and continued in fashion under that name until about 1450; thereafter being simply called the 'gown'. It was a new type of garment put on over the head, and apart from minor details, was made in the following way. From narrow shoulders there was a gradual sloping outwards and downwards into deep tubular folds which were held in place at the waist by the girdle. It was made in four pieces with seams at the back, front and sides. The seams were left open a short length from the hem, forming vents. It could be any length: long to the ground for ceremonial occasions, or short to knee-length. The neckline had a high standing collar, spreading out, reaching to the ears. Sometimes it was high at the back, merging with the head-wear with an edge scalloped in a close dagging. The collar was fastened either with buttons or with hooks and eyes. When the collar was left undone, it was slightly turned down.

Towards the end of the century the houppelande was often buttoned down the front. The sleeves were funnel shaped, sloping from the shoulders downwards, and finishing in a large opening, the lowest edge often reaching down to the ground. The top edge came only to the wrist, the hand being left uncovered. The sleeves were ornamented with dagging.

Long houppelande with sewn-in folds and close-fitting sleeves. The gipon can be seen through the side opening of the houppelande (c.1413).

Short tunic with a baldrick and girdle with follybells attached (c.1450).

This type of decoration, often called 'jagging', was very fashionable from the late fourteenth century until about 1500, although it was first seen towards the end of the twelfth century. Appliqué work was sometimes added. The houppelande was decorated along the hem, as were the slits of the skirt, round the edge of the sleeve aperture and round the top edge of the collar, which gave a ruff-like appearance. The shoulder pieces or epaulettes were also dagged and ornamented with embroidery. Outer clothes such as cloaks remained in fashion until the end of the century. They were then used mainly for travelling. The profusely dagged, short cape was popular from about 1330 to 1430, and thereafter became unfashionable. Knee-length capes which were buttoned from neck to hem with a low collar were often worn.

FOOTWEAR

The soled hose remained in vogue. Eyelet holes at the top border, which reached the fork, were strung with estaches to the underside of the gipon. The hose were cut on the cross from an elasticated type of material, the seam running down the back. The hose were parti-coloured until about the first quarter of the fourteenth century. The feet of the hose were shaped to the foot, the chief characteristic being the point opposite the big toe, which was increased in size. From the late fourteenth century (about 1395) until the early fifteenth century (about 1410), pointed toes became more exaggerated and were known as *long pikes* or *cracowes*. These pikes were stuffed with various materials, such as wool, tow, moss and even hay.

During the middle of the century (about 1360) shoes became sharply pointed with punched-out designs. The long pike shoes in these early times were at first banned under a sumptuary law of Edward III (1327–1377); the penalty being fines levied on both maker and wearer. But by about 1395, the long spear-like pikes, or *poulaines*, came into fashionable wear. The higher the nobility, the longer the point permitted. Eventually even boots followed the fashion of the long pike style. The new type fastening for short boots with hooks on the outer side was introduced in about 1395. Galoshes and clogs were worn by many. Wooden-soled *pattens* came into use, these being attached to the shoes with leather straps. They were used to protect the footwear from the filthy conditions of the highways.

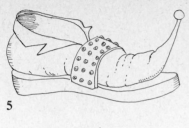

5

6

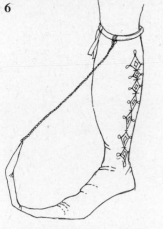

1 *Long-toed leather shoe with side lacing.*

2 *Stirrup-type hose.*

3 *Rose window patterned shoe.*

4 *Shoe known as 'poulaine', long pointed toe attached to front with chain and tassels.*

5 *Long-toed, bell tipped with wooden pattern, with a jewelled or decorated leather strap.*

6 *Extreme toe length type called a 'cracowe', the ornamentation up the sides was sometimes jewelled, and these were the first 'clocks'.*

HEAD-WEAR

The liripipe hood was still extensively worn. The wearing of the hood-turban changed in style and character. The face opening was changed to fit on the head; the previous neck edge was pulled back into a roll and the long liripipe was turned and twisted round the crown, the loose end left to hang down one side. The gorget, which was in folds, hung to the opposite side. If it was made of a stiffer material able to stand upright, fanwise over the head, the dagged edge standing proud like a cockerel's comb, although this varied according to the fashion fads of the wearer.

The earlier style of hats and coifs continued to be in fashionable wear, with the exception of added ornamentation and trimmings. Dyed feathers became part of the decorative design of hats. This plumage was worn in the front, back or sides, at the wearer's desire and was fastened on with jewelled ornaments. The lavishly decorated hatbands became popular. Rings were often attached to the hats, which allowed them to be slung at the back. Gold head circlets were worn by the nobility.

Newer styles of head-wear were emerging, but did not become common until the following century.

HAIR STYLES

Hair styles changed very little. Hair was worn either long or short to the lower part of the neck from a centre parting, or was reasonably short without a parting. In the 1350s it was brushed forward into an uneven fringe, the sides ending in a roll at chin or shoulder level. If beards were worn they were forked into two or three points, but the clean-shaven look remained very popular.

Towards the end of the century the styles became more elaborate with the hair combed back with bunches of curls either side of the face. By the fourteenth century both hair and beards became longer, being worn either in long flowing tresses, or, as was popular with the younger generations, turned under or cut in a straight fringe with the sides being curled behind the ears.

ACCESSORIES

Gloves were now very popular and worn by all classes. Hand-cloths, hand-coverchiefs, or mokadors, were beginning to appear.

It is interesting to note that about the middle of the fourteenth century the colour black became the accepted colour for sorrow. At first only one black garment was worn over the ordinary clothes. Initially this was confined to the nobility and upper class. Pouches, purses, keys and daggers, hanging from the girdles, were carried as accessories.

Female styles

GOWN
The second half of the century continued with the gown being close fitting at the bodice from which the skirt hung in full folds. The girdle was worn at hip level. The sleeves, close fitting to the wrist and widening over the hand to the knuckles, were fastened above or below the elbow to the wrist by buttons.

OUTER–GARMENTS
The cote-hardie remained as in the first half of the century, but was now closely following the men's fashions in the sleeve style: the short, hanging flaps changed to long dangling pieces called *tippets*. These then became longer than the fashionable male style, almost trailing to the ground. Girdles were not worn unless the gown was replaced by the cote-hardie beneath the sideless surcote.

The sideless surcote was a development of the sleeveless surcote, the most characteristic feature being the long side openings from the shoulders to the hips, revealing the girdle beneath the undergarment. The front section, which gave the stomacher effect, curved to the waist and was usually shaped to a round hem below, making a change in form. This was known as a *plackard* and was often made of fur. The skirt section fell to the ground from the hips in loose folds. The neckline was wide and deep, the bodice part hanging on by shoulder straps, then made secure by fastening the gown underneath the plackard. The plackard was often decorated with buttons or jewels down the centre front. Fur edging and lavish lining was very popular. Long, sleeveless surcoats with side vents were worn either as domestic garments or by the lower classes. Mantles were now mainly ceremonial, being highly decorated and fastened loosely across the breast by tasselled cords or jewelled bands. Hooded cloaks were used for travelling, which also, of course, entailed riding. The ladies and nobility rode side-saddle, while the country women

A dagged cape sometimes worn separately with the liripipe hood which was wound round the head (c.1360).

The sideless surcoat was without sleeves and was open to hip level, close fitting at the top and falling to a long, full-folded skirt. The hair was arranged into coils over the ears. The wimple and fret were still a popular fashion (1310–1340).

The cote-hardie style remained popular with the middle class. The wide cuff at the elbow revealed the slashed sleeve of the under-garment. The wimple also remained in fashion with the middle class (c.1380).

rode in the male fashion, astride.

The short pelissons still maintained their place in fashion. The unusual posture of pushing forward the stomach and curving the back in a slouching position was affected by the most fashionable ladies. Leg-wear continued as in the beginning of the century, supported with garters. Footwear generally followed the same fashion as for men, but the style of the long pikes never became part of women's fashion.

HEADDRESS AND HAIR STYLES

For head-gear, the wimples and the veils continued in common use, the veil becoming more ornamental. A newer style called the *goffered veil* came into fashion in about 1370. Made in linen, it was cut in a semi-circle and placed over the head, several layers at a time, the front edge being ornamental with a goffered frill, not unlike the later ruffs. This framed the face in an arch effect, sometimes ending at ear level or just below the chin, or it fell to shoulder level, where it again became goffered and draped round the shoulders.

Ornamental fillets with side pieces resembling open-worked carved pillars, decorated the sides of the head on either side in front of the ears, making a very square-faced effect. Inside these pillars, side hair pieces were drawn through. The hair was then covered with a net or veil which draped down the back. Ornamental fillets were also worn without side pieces, sometimes even without a fret or veils. Side-positioned, vertical hair plaits occasionally were worn in place of the 'carved side pillars'. The fillet styles merged towards the end of the century, making way for the more complicated and elaborate styles of the next century.

Also towards the end of the century was the *chaplet* style, which was a stuffed roll worn over a fret or caul. For ordinary usage was the hood and hat fashion, the former used mainly for travelling. Hair remained concealed either partially or completely under the veil, but it was coiled or braided around the ears. It was fashionable to wear the hair in vertical plaits, straight down to the cheeks to just below the ears, the ends being returned and hidden under the head covering.

Hair could also be worn by having a centre parting with the plaits placed horizontally round the head, the wimple fastened underneath, and the lower edge tucked into the gown at the neck. Plaits were allowed to hang down, towards the middle of the fourteenth century. Vertical plaits remained in fashion until the end of the Plantagenet period (1399) and the hair was covered by a veil with a gold or silver fillet with false hair attached. The fillet could be adorned with jewels. This style developed from the crespine and later, with further embellishments, became an important style of head-dress in the fifteenth century. Side cauls made into cylinder shape by flexible wire were worn, one either side of the head, with the hair either loose or plaited and placed through the open tops and left hanging down in front of the ears. These cauls were attached to the projections of a fillet or coronet and were decorated with jewels.

From 1370 until the fifteenth century a semi-circular veil became popular, the straight edge framing the face and the remainder being allowed to hang loose. The face was framed with a goffered edging.

From about 1380, side hair was puffed out and covered by a net bag, each side attached to a fillet. Over this was worn a padded and decorated roll with a veil hanging down behind.

The new fashion of shaving the front hair, giving a high broad forehead effect, came in towards the end of the century and continued in fashion until late in the fifteenth century (1370–1480).

ACCESSORIES

The mode of using lavish make-up and the plucking of eyebrows became very common among the upper classes. The use of dagging as ornamentation was not used as often on the female costume. The wearing of jewellery, decorative effects and the use of a brighter and wider variety of colours became more pronounced.

The wimple suspended from the hair with a silken band around the head (c.1350).

The front of the veil edged with several layers of ruffles and goffering (c.1365).

Plain veil and wimple covering the plaited coils on either side of the head (c.1345).

Hair enclosed in fouriaux suspended from a band worn around the head, complete with veil (c.1345).

TOP LEFT: *Traveller with hood or cowl which developed into the liripipe(c.1310).*

TOP RIGHT: *Lady with shaven forehead wearing a truncated hennin and veil style(c.1455).*

BOTTOM LEFT: *Under- and over-tunic fashion worn with a wimple and caul head-dress(c.1325).*

BOTTOM RIGHT: *A knight of the Crusades(c.1195).*

LEFT: *Saxon theyn wearing the Phrygian cap and basic tunic, hose and cloak.*

CENTRE: *Saxon peasant woman with her long gown drawn up over the short under-garment.*

RIGHT: *Saxon peasant with the same basic clothes as the theyn, tunic and hose, and the legs covered with strips of cloth.*

Under the Red Rose: The House of Lancaster (1399–1461)

The round chaplet covered with dagged leaf shapes was popular with both men and women (c. 1410).

Soft, high-crowned hat with a rolled brim, the crown being pulled forward (c.1410).

A soft, high-crowned hat with a rolled brim (c.1412).

Male styles

DOUBLET

From the beginning of the fifteenth century, the word 'doublet' came into general use and was maintained over a very long period until about 1670. It was a close-fitting, waisted garment, cut close to the hips, not quite reaching the thighs. It was well stuffed with padding, this being built up more over the chest. It was cut and made up from eight pieces of material, with a centre seam at the back and round the waist. The fastenings, i.e. lacing, buttons, or hooks and eyes, were down the centre front. The neckline continued to be cut round and without a collar until about 1420. After this date collars were added. They were at first close fitting, then varied from stand-up styles with a V-shaped slit in front, or cut with points under the chin, to being fastened by lacing across, which was the style from about 1450 to 1490.

Round the hem of the doublet were now inserted 'eyelet holes', which had their counterpart round the upper edge of the hose. Through these eyelet holes were threaded ties, or 'points' as they were known, to attach the doublet to the hose. Materials, such as broadcloth, linen, leather, satin, velvet and damask, were used in the making of the doublet. The quilting was held together by stitching in a variety of ways: vertical, which was favoured by the military, horizontal or invisible. If the doublet was worn alone, a belt was worn at hip level. Sleeves were tight fitting to the wrist, then extended over the knuckles, buttoning up to elbow level.

Grandes-assiettes sleeves were still worn, although they were becoming uncommon.

OUTER-GARMENTS

The cote-hardie, now usually called a 'jacket', continued to be close fitting to the body and tight-waisted, shaped with gatherings both in the front and at the back. No fastenings were visible as these were placed under the pleatings. Until about 1410, the jacket was very short, reaching only to the fork or crutch. It then became knee length. The neckline was surmounted by a stand-up collar from 1380 to 1420. After this date the jacket became collarless, as the collar was now attached to the doublet. Sleeves varied, but the tight-fitting buttoned-to-the-elbow style with the bugle cuffs, which extended to the knuckles, became popular. Belts were worn at hip level.

The liripipe chaperon, now made in three sections, the burlet, gorget and liripipe (c.1440).

HOUPPELANDE

Although structurally the same, the gown, or houppelande, began to have many changes in detail. After about 1440 and lasting well into the next century, when there were no vents present, it was known as a 'closed gown' with an open front, fastened from the neckline to the hem with either hooks and eyes or buttons. These fastenings were hidden beneath the pleated folds which were sewn down under the belt. Until about 1440 the usual method of pleating was with eight folds, being in pairs at the front, at the back and on either side. From this date on the folds were heavily pleated down the front and back with the sides plain. The neckline had a collar which stood proud and high, often dagged and fastened with buttons from chin to hem (1380–1410). Also fashionable at this time was a similar version of the gown with a slightly lower collar and a V-shaped opening at the neck. This became unfashionable in about 1425. A large, turned-down collar which lay flat over the shoulders also became unfashionable at the same period.

From about 1425 the shallow upright collar which sloped to a broad V-shape at the throat came into fashion, closely following the style of the collar of the doublet which came over it. This was a vogue which persisted until about 1460 regardless of the newer collarless style being worn to the end of the century. Fur was the most common material for the edging of the neckline, irrespective of whether it was summer or winter. The shape of the neckline varied from about 1420

Low-crowned hat with turned-up brim worn over the hood (c.1430).

Brimless turkey bonnet with small stalk, c. 1460.

Musician of c. 1460.

to 1480. It was close fitting in front with a V-shape behind. From 1450 to 1470 a similar style was fashionable, but with a U-shape at the back. Popular, from time to time, was the V-shape neckline which was both in the front and at the back. A V-shape neckline sloping in front was fashionable from about 1430 to 1465. Most commonplace was the round neck, which continued to be popular from 1425 to 1500.

The sleeves followed three fashionable styles: open, closed or hanging. The latter style was either open or closed. The open sleeve was in a large funnel-shaped style which remained in fashion up to 1420, and for ceremonial occasions until 1450. Throughout the period, 1400–1500, the cylindrical sleeve with the same dimensions from the shoulder to the wrist, was worn, reaching a great fashionable popularity in about 1430. A style similar to the cylindrical shape, but shortened by turning it back on itself giving a large cuffed effect and a lining in a contrasting colour, was worn off and on during the period between 1400 and 1480. The closed-sleeve style remained in common use with variations to beyond the end of the century. The sleeve was cut in one piece with a seam down the front and fastened with buttons at the wrist. It was full and gathered into a wrist cuff, or simply shaped to the wrist without a cuff.

From about 1410 the very wide sleeve with a hanging-bag effect, called a 'bagpipe sleeve' or 'pokys', was worn. This became unfashionable in the 1430s. After 1445 a much fuller version appeared, which had a 'kick-up' effect at the shoulder.

The hanging sleeve, in many variations, lasted until the 1520s. The sleeves had an opening down the front of the upper arm which permitted the sleeved doublet to be passed through. Very popular during the early part of the century was the 'closed sleeve' which was very wide and full and gathered into a cuff. Long cylindrical-type sleeves were known as 'open sleeves' (i.e. open at the wrist).

Houppelandes were made in various materials such as wool, satin, damask. The edges were usually trimmed with fur – sable, fox, lamb, ermine and beaver for the nobility and squirrel, rabbit and even cat for the lower class. The garment was usually lined, the lining being governed by the seasons. In summer linen, satin or silk was used, whereas in winter a fur or heavier cloth was employed.

GIRDLE

Throughout the early part of the century a girdle or belt was always worn. It was considered a sign of disgrace for a man to be seen without his belt. Only as a sign or symbol of penance or humility was a beltless gown worn. Belts were worn around the hips from about 1400, but this became uncommon after 1460. The most popular fashion trend was to wear the belt around the waist from this period until the end of the century. Belts were made of leather or silk in a variety of colours, such as red, blue, black and white. Buckles as central fasteners were of gold, silver, copper or iron, and were made in a variety of shapes. Often belts were tied into knots after passing through the buckle, with the long trailing ends hanging down in front to just below knee length. Suspended from the belts were pouches or wallets made of leather, often with a dagger fixed to the back of the pouch. If no pouch was worn, the dagger was attached to the belt by means of a small chain or sling.

CLOAKS

The cloak continued to be worn until the middle of the century when it gradually became unfashionable. The dagged shoulder cape, which was worn without the hood and had retained its popularity for 100 years (1330–1430), was seldom worn by the fashionable upper class after 1430. The military-style *huke*, which originally was worn over armour, was worn as a replacement for the cloak in the first half of the century. The tabard-style huke was put on over the head, and was worn over the doublet in the summer and over the gown in the winter. For riding, the huke was cut short to mid-thigh and slit up the front. For ordinary wear it fell to below knee length and was worn without the slit in the front. The longer ground-length version of the huke became fashionable after the 1550s.

FOOTWEAR

Two types of hose continued to be worn. The separate stocking type retained its popularity, especially with the lower class. They were long with a tongued top edge for attaching to the doublet. The border was made with eyelet holes, through which ties were passed to corresponding ones in the doublet. This procedure was called 'trussing the points'. The ties were known as *points* or *herlots*. Because the points were inclined to break, labourers never used them for back fastenings, but often rolled the stockings down to just below

A cote-hardie, short with houppelande-style sleeves and neck (c. 1380).

52

the knees. When working in warmer weather and in the fields, braies were the usual form of leg-wear.

The joined-hose was a combination of stockings and braies into a single garment, similar to modern tights. These were usually worn with shorter cut clothes.

At the beginning of the fifteenth century, the two legs, which reached to the crotch, were joined and came up over the hips, just covering the seat. Later in the century they continued higher to reach the waist. Similar to the separate hose, they were pierced along the top border with eyelet holes in pairs which corresponded to similar pairs around the lower border of the doublet. The ties, which joined the doublet and hose, were usually made of leather with metal end pieces called *aiglets*. The eyelet holes in both the hose and the doublet varied in number from two to 12 pairs, the most popular number being nine, two pairs in front, three pairs at each side, and one pair at the back.

The *cod piece*, which came into fashion in the early part of the century, was a small bag with a flap at the fork of the hose, closed by ties. The name 'cod' was Old English for 'bag'.

Hose, usually made of woollen material reinforced with leather and often lined, were made in bright colours.

Both the separate and joined hose could be footed, worn with stirrups, or worn without shoes. Wooden and leather pattens were worn in inclement weather. The piked, long, stuffed points shaped to the foot went out of fashion in the 1410s. They became round at the toe for a short period, and then returned to the pointed toe until 1460. In the 1480s the long pike reappeared.

Short, boot-buskins were worn throughout the century; close fitting and calf length, they were fastened by lacing, hooks and eyes or buckles slightly to the side of the centre.

Shoes were usually made in one piece, with a seam running down the back. Also popular was the long buskin boot which became very fashionable from the middle of the century for other than just horse riding. They were high to the thigh, tight fitting with a slit at the knee to enable the knee to bend at the joint. The buskins could be fastened either on the inner or the outer side. Special socks were worn over the hose when wearing the buskins. The shape of the foot followed the fashionable mode of the period. Footwear was usually made from hide, goat, cow or sheep skins. The country people wore a gaiter legging which was fastened with ties just below

Long full skirt gathered on to hip-length surcoate (c. 1380).

the knee and around the ankle.

Shoes continued throughout the century in the same basic styles, being cut similar to low boots, covering the foot and clinging to the ankle. The early style of the open shoe with an ankle strap fastening was becoming unfashionable. The wooden-soled pattens remained in common use throughout the century. They were usually made from aspen wood which was ideal as it was lightweight. Fastening was by means of black leather straps which were nailed on either side, came over the instep and secured by buckles. The most popular period for these was from 1440 to 1460.

The richer classes wore boots known as *boteurs*. These reached the thighs, and were made of soft leather and lined in a contrasting colour with the tops turned down. They were fastened with a jewelled clasp buckle just under the knees.

HEAD-WEAR

The hood, which had given long service to fashionable garments, finally went out of favour in the middle of the century (1450) although worn with a closed gorget and liripipe it continued in fashion until about 1480. However a small hood which was fastened by buttons in front, and pushed back to give a muffler effect, was very popular. The hood turban continued to be worn, but it underwent some changes and was now called a *chaperon* (1420–1470). This consisted of three sections, the burlet, gorget and liripipe, which were sewn together. The burlet was a round, stuffed roll pad and into this was sewn the gorget which was taken from round the neck to the crown of the head. In its transformed position the gorget could be placed into either of two positions. The first, if it were stiffened, could stand upright like a cockerel's comb, sloping from one side to the other. The end of the comb hung over one side of the burlet with the liripipe hanging over the other. The second, if the gorget were limp, the mass of material hung down in folds over the side while the liripipe counter-balanced the structure by hanging over the opposite side. When the liripipe was not included, the folds of the gorget hung down the back of the head from ear to ear.

Chaperons and hats with liripipes attached were often carried hanging over the left shoulder, with the liripipe in front and the hat hanging behind. A skullcap replaced the coif for wearing under any other head-wear. A large variety of hats were worn.

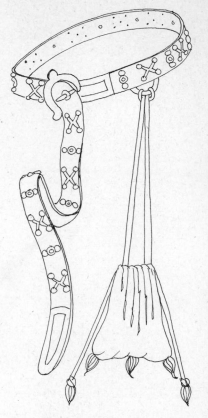

Ornamental girdle with tasselled bag.

Man's money pouch worn on a belt.

Long centre-parted hairstyle of c. 1480.

Until the period of 1415 the 'top hat', a tall hat which tapered upwards to a broad top with a wide rolled brim, was fashionable. The bag-shaped floppy crown style, which allowed the crown to fall either sideways or forwards over a rolled brim, was popular in the 1430s. During the same period the Robin-Hood type hat was also both fashionable and popular. This had a low tapering crown with a long peaked brim turned up at the back. Also common was the tall crowned hat with the spiked top shaped like a hour glass, which had a broad brim that could be worn either turned up or down, depending on the wearer's taste. This was popular from about 1430 to 1440. From this period to the 1460s the balloon-crowned hat, which was very large and had a fairly wide brim slightly turned up or down, was worn. The high cone-shaped crown with the brim turned up all round, or turned up at the back and down at the front, or vice versa, was popular between 1445 and 1485. Hats were usually made from beaver with both rough and smooth surfaces, and often lined with velvet or satin. Both hats and linings were in various colours. Decorations for hats consisted of fur, feather plumes, decorated hat bands, precious and semi-precious jewels, buckles and brooches.

HAIR STYLES

The characteristic style of the 'bowl-cut' hair style remained in fashion from 1410 to 1460, and in some rare cases up to 1480. The hair was shaped into a narrow skull cap effect, with the lower part of the hair just level to the top of the ears. Below this level the head and the neck were closely shaven. From the crown of the head the hair was brushed out to form a thick circular fringe completely around the head. With this style of haircut it was usual to have a clean-shaven face, a fashion lasting from 1415 to 1525. Forked or pointed beards were worn early in the century (1400–1414) but they were unfashionable with the short haircut.

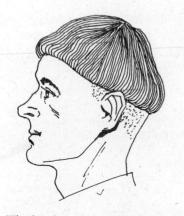

The bowl-cut hairstyle, the hair shaved up to the level of the ears, being combed down from the crown of the head and the ends curled under (1410–1460).

ACCESSORIES

In the early part of the century until 1410 fashionable accessories included the knightly girdles made of joined metal clasps, worn at hip level by the nobility. The jewelled collars were in common use from 1400 to 1550. Decorative bells, which hung from neck bands, shoulder belts or from the girdle, were fashionable with the younger people. From the girdle were slung pouches, keys, or daggers. Gloves and walking sticks were worn and carried.

Female styles

KIRTLE

The fifteenth century can be seen as a transition from the Middle Ages to the Renaissance. Brilliant colours were used and unusual costumes and headdresses were worn. The female silhouette became longer with a higher waistline. The *kirtle*, or tunic, was worn over the smock. It was close fitting and low necked with long, close-fitting sleeves, often reaching over the hand to the knuckles. The sleeve fastening was usually from the elbow to the wrist with buttons. The kirtle itself was buttoned or laced down the centre front from the neckline to just below the waist, although sometimes it was laced at the back.

OUTER-GARMENT

The cote-hardie was worn until about the 1450s, but was often concealed or even replaced by the houppelande, which had become fashionable at the beginning of the century.

The houppelande, known now as the 'gown', was popular from the early 1400s to the 1450s. Like its male counterpart, the female houppelande had assumed all the uses of a gown, and apart from minor differences, they were identical. For the female, the girdle was worn in a high-waisted position, and the gown was always worn long to the ground. On ceremonial occasions the gown had a train, often of great length.

During the early part of the century the houppelande had a high-necked collar reaching up to the ears. As the garment was put on over the head, the neck opening was buttoned up from the breast to the chin. Sometimes the collar was left open in a high V-shaped opening or the top buttons were left unfastened and the collar turned down slightly (1400–1410). Also worn during this period was the wide, flat, turned-down collar with a V-shape opening or fastened by lacing from the neck to the bosom. Sometimes this type of collar was made of fur (1400–1440). The broad V-shape opening at the front and back and descending to the girdle became popular later. The opening was edged with lapels which followed the shape of the 'V' by narrowing towards the girdle. The opening revealed the under-garment, either the kirtle or the cote-hardie. The neckline was bare, from about 1440 to 1460.

Woman's belt with purse and keys (c.14th century).

Light veil worn over the hair enclosed in a caul (c.1405).

Informal wear of the hair dressed up on either side of the head and the head covered with a small, pleated linen veil (c.1400).

The early turban style head-dress covered by a light linen veil (c.1410).

The decorated roll type hat over the reticulated caul (c.1405).

The sleeves of the gown were again similar to those of the male garment, but the large, funnel-shaped sleeve remained in fashion longer with female attire than that of the male (1400 to 1460). The plain, tubular sleeve remained in fashion from about 1400 to 1470. The bagpipe style lasted only from 1400 until 1430 and then became unfashionable. The long, tubular, hanging sleeve of the open style was fashionable from 1430 to 1500.

CLOAKS

Cloaks in the early part of the century followed the style of the houppelande, being made with high collars to cover the collar of the gown (1400–1410). Hooded cloaks were worn but generally only for travelling. The hood itself was fashionable until about 1450, and thereafter less so. It was sometimes worn open with side flaps which stood out. These projections were called after the French, *oreilliettes*, meaning 'ears', which they resembled. For the wealthier classes the hoods were often lined with fur, miniver being very popular. The attachment of the liripipe for the female hood was often a complicated arrangement, it was cut vertically and turned back, then fastened down the centre at the back of the hood so that at the bend, two small projections appeared, giving a horned effect.

HEADDRESS AND HAIR

It was during this period that new and sometimes elaborate styles of head-dress made their appearance. To suit these fashionable new styles the hair was often concealed, and in certain instances, was shaved off above the forehead. Head-gear became wider reaching a peak in the 1430s, then becoming unfashionable by the 1450s. The chaplet headdress was an irregular, thick, stuffed ring-shape, pulled and stretched out on either side. Following the male fashion, it was dagged and decorated with a jewel in the centre front. This was worn over a net that concealed the hair which was coiled to form a bosse-shape at either side of the temples. Materials varied with the seasons: heavy for the winter and lighter for spring and summer.

Next in fashion came the wide shapes with side attachments just above the ears and called *templers*, from the French *templettes*. These rounded, templer attachments enclosed the hair at the temples, and were made of gold and sometimes jewelled. The net or gauze worn under the ornamental fillet or coronet formed a draping which hung down behind. Following this fashion was an even wider style. The ornamental fillet had templers which covered the ears and extended outwards in various widths to suit the taste of the wearer. The head-wear itself became wider to accommodate the templers. The headdress now became more elaborate and ornamental. By 1416 the templers developed into enormous shapes in the form of cow horns. This style became known as the *horned headdress*. This style was worn with a fine veiling which was stretched outwards and above the templers with a back draping which fell in folds down the back to the shoulders. The horn shape became higher, then changed direction inwards forming a heart-shaped headdress. The side pieces formed a U-shape above the forehead. A short veil draped the structure from 1420 to 1450. Now taller shapes became fashionable and the headdress was worn without the templers or side projections. The sausage-shaped roll, which was arched up on either side into a U-shape over the forehead and back of the head, became popular. This style was placed above the ears and worn with a backward tilt. The front hair was shaven off, as were the eyebrows, to give a high, clear forehead effect. Often with this style a gorget and liripipe were added as decoration (1445–1460).

Popular was the open-crown circular headdress of the turban style reputed to have been brought back by the Crusaders after the capture of Constantinople in 1453. The turban consisted of a lightweight frame covered in a fine material, embellished with stars and crescent shapes. This also increased in height and was worn with and without a veil from about 1440 to 1480. With this fashion the hair could be worn long, coming through the centre opening and allowed to hang down, long and flowing. With other headgear the hair was usually confined.

A horned-type headdress covered with veils. A wimple was often worn with this style (1413–1422).

The decorated roll with a U-shaped dip over a reticulated caul (c.1410).

FOOTWEAR
Stockings were short and gartered just below or above the knees. Shoes followed the male fashion, but were shorter during the excessively piked period.

ACCESSORIES
Jewellery followed closely that of the male styles as did most other accessories such as gloves and carrying pouches. Short aprons without bibs were worn for most domestic chores.

A short veil worn over the reticulated caul held on with a head-band (c.1415).

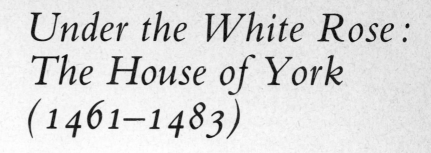

Under the White Rose: The House of York (1461–1483)

The doublet open in front was laced loosely together. It had a full sleeve, which was close fitting at the wrist and was slashed just below the elbow. The long gown was open down the front with a broad collar, long sleeves with a large slash in front. The hose was fitted with a cod-piece (c.1485).

Male styles

DOUBLET

During the second half of the fifteenth century the doublet remained close fitting, fully padded and waisted and extremely short, not quite covering the hips. By 1485 it ended just above waist level, sometimes without the skirt section. Fastening was down the centre front with lacing ties, buttons or hooks and eyes. Between 1450 and 1490 the neckline had a high stand-up collar with a wide V-shape opening in the front, which gradually became broader and deeper, showing the chemise or shirt top. Over this, the collar was fastened by lacing ties. Sleeves remained close fitting to the wrist, but now were often just tied on at the armholes and were, therefore, detachable. This was in vogue from 1450 to 1500. The simple, slashed-across-the-elbow sleeve, through which was pulled the shirt sleeve, was worn during the period from 1480 to 1500. This was the forerunner of a later popular fashion. Doublets were usually made in velvet and linen.

PETTICOAT

From 1450 to 1515 the petticoat came into fashion. This was a waisted type of garment, short and well padded, which was worn over the shirt and under the doublet. Adopted for warmth it was close fitting with a rounded neck which was cut lower at the back and was fitted with or without close-fitting sleeves.

JACKET

The jacket, or jerkin, replaced the cote-hardie in about 1450. This was cut either to mid-thigh with side vents, or came above the hips revealing the seat. Following the doublet style it was close fitting and waisted with a full skirt which flared outwards during the period 1450–1480. The fashionable trend was to have vertical pleats both front and back of the bodice and skirt, shaped fanwise and radiating from the centre of the waist. The side panels were plain without folds.

A fashion, which came into being in the 1480s, was to wear a jacket with gathers and a separate longer skirt, known as a 'base'. This became more popular in the early sixteenth century until about 1540. The wide shoulder effect, characteristic of the period, for jackets and gowns was created by the use of shoulder pads or *mahoitres*. The sleeves were gathered over these pads to the shoulder seam. The neckline had no collar and was a round-cut shape with a short, wide V-opening in the front or at the back, or a narrow V-shape in the front to the waist (1450–1480). In 1480–1490, a deeper V-shape opening in the centre front to the waist, revealing the doublet, was worn. Sometimes a separate piece, known as a 'stomacher', was inserted in the opening. The sleeves were either closed, open or hanging. When closed, they were full at the shoulders and narrowed down to the wrist, plain and buttoned or were full throughout and gathered on to a wrist band. The full sleeve was usually slashed and laced vertically, showing the under-sleeve of the garment. The open sleeve was full at the shoulder, tubular in shape and tapered slightly to the wrist.

Sometimes the sleeve was turned back to the elbow, giving a short sleeve effect. The different coloured lining gave a deep cuff appearance. The long, hanging sleeves were in the form of a wide tube which dropped to just below the knees. Sometimes these sleeves were joined together at the back to keep them out of the way. The slit for the arms was very wide.

The jacket materials were of leather, velvet, fustian or figured satin, which under a sumptuary law of Edward IV (1461–1483) was only allowed to be worn by persons above the rank of knight. The lining was usually of linen or a thicker cloth.

GOWN

The houppelande, now known as the gown, changed very little except when worn long, then it had either a side or rear

The above-knee-length jerkin had full sleeves fastening at the wrists. The gown, just below knee length was open down the front with a broad, fur collar. The sleeves were also edged in fur at the cuff, and were slit down the centre. A small round hat with a turned-up brim was also popular (c.1483).

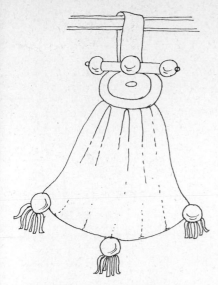

Typical three-tassel purses, gypciere, attached to girdle (1485–1490).

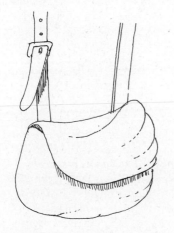

Shoulder bag worn for travelling (1485–1490).

vent. *Demi-gown* was the name given to the knee-length gown. The pleats were arranged in massed vertical folds, at the front and back. They were secured in place by stitching at the waist which concealed the join with a belt. The sides remained plain without folds. The fastening was usually down the centre front with hooks and eyes, but was very often pulled over in a double-breasted style. The padded mahoîtres were still very popular. The fashionable, short-standing collar with the rounded edges, sloping to a V-shape in the front, continued to be worn during the period 1425 to 1460. The collarless style, with variations, continued throughout the century. The V-shape in the front was popular between 1430 and 1465 and the V-shape at the back from 1430 to 1480. A U-shaped collar was fashionable from 1450 to 1470. The round neckline continued to be worn from 1425 until 1500. The square-cut collar, flat at the back and coming over the shoulders in a wide lapel style continuing down to the front hem line and sometimes faced with fur, was very popular from 1485–1540.

The girdle was optional during the latter half of the century. If it was worn, it was usually a narrow silk ribbon. The sleeves were either the open or closed variety. When open, they were usually plain and cylindrical in shape (1415–1485). Closed, they were usually full and gathered at the shoulder and shaped or gathered at the wrist (1405–1500). Another kind of open sleeve was the hanging type with an opening down the front seam (1430–1625). Fur edgings were still very popular.

Characteristic of the period was the 'Pedestrian tabard', which had ground-length front and back panels. This was often worn with only the front panel secured by a belt; the back one was allowed to hang free. Sometimes sleeves were added which were either fur-trimmed or dagged. Cloaks, although worn, were not fashionable wear and were used mainly for extra warmth or for travelling. Thigh-length capes, occasionally with hoods, were worn.

FOOTWEAR

The hose reached up to the waist in about 1475. The seat section, now called 'breeches', was often different both in colour and material to that of the leg parts. Striped hose and parti-coloured hose were back in fashion in about 1485. The method of fastening remained by trussing the hose to the doublet or waistcoat, or petticoat. Also maintaining its position in fashion was the cod-piece. Thick, loose-fitting overstockings, which were shaped to the feet, were sometimes worn, usually turned down at the knees.

Between 1450 and 1500 long boots or buskins were very popular. These thigh-length boots could be laced on either the inner or outer side of the leg. The tops were often turned down to give a deep turn over. Shorter buskins were also in common use. The style in points changed: from 1450 to 1460, the short points were fashionable; from 1460 to 1480 the piked style; and the really shorter points were worn from 1480 until 1490. Shoes also varied in style from high-cut, round-the-ankle to the deep V-cut shape on either side. This gave a long, pointed tongue in front over the ankles, with a similar tongue shape at the back of the ankles. Pattens remained in fashion; the peak period being from 1440 to 1460.

HEAD-WEAR

The hood continued to be worn, especially when riding. The chaperon was a fashionable hood until about 1470.

Throughout the century the bowler-style hat with the round crown and the curled-up brim remained in fashion. A most popular fashion was to have an upright feather either at the front or at the back attached to the hat by some jewel or ornament (1400–1500). Straw hats of simple design and shapes were very common. Bonnets or caps, not unlike a fez, in various heights were popular during the period of 1450 to 1485, and were known as *turkey bonnets*. The flat pork-pie bonnets with a turned-up brim were popular from 1475 to 1500.

HAIR STYLES

The *bowl-crop* hair style continued to be worn in its short form from 1410 until 1460. The longer style of the bowl crop now slightly covered the forehead and the back of the neck (1450–1475). Most popular and fashionable was the 'pageboy' style. This had a fringed forehead piece either waved or straight or with a centre parting. The hair hung down to either neck or shoulder level, being waved or left straight. Hair was kept tidy with the aid of resin and egg white. In the fifteenth century hair could be worn in most styles and colours. The *florentine cut*, a curly shoulder-length hairstyle was very popular. Light-coloured wigs, sometimes made with the addition of horsehair, were very popular.

Men and women dyed their hair blond with saffron or onion skins. Although blond hair was the most popular colour of the period, black was also favoured. Red hair was considered unlucky.

The face was usually left clean shaven for the fashionable men and beards were not popular, although worn by older men in a variety of styles, rounded, pointed or double-pointed.

ACCESSORIES

Common accessories for this period were the heavily jewelled necklaces, especially in the first half of the fifteenth century. Handcoverchiefs or handkerchiefs were carried. A breast coverchief or stomacher coverchief was worn over the shirt at breast level.

A *muckinder* was a lower class or child's handkerchief made of linen and used as a table napkin.

Gloves were popular and the import of them from abroad was forbidden by Edward in 1463, no doubt to protect British manufacturers.

Pikes or pouches, a kind of detachable pocket, were carried. Most fashionable was the *gypciere*. This was a large purse with three tassels, which was drawn in at the top and then attached to the girdle by a strap.

On ceremonial occasions the nobility wore a broad, jewelled shoulder belt called a *baldrick*, and 'folly bells' were worn by the younger men, either on the waistband or from a shoulder belt. Walking sticks or staves, some being quite long, were carried.

Female styles

KIRTLE

During the last period of the fifteenth century (1450–1490) the kirtle, although it continued in use, was seldom seen. The over-garment or gown, which had earlier been called the houppelande, was now the favourite fashionable attire. Because of its variance of style both the old and newer styles overlapped. The tubular folds gave way to a new, loose-flowing style with a fairly high waistline, which gave plenty of width round the hem of the ground-length skirt. The fashion of long trains became very common. The bodice of the gown which had earlier been gathered at the waist now fitted much closer to the figure. The revers were placed off the shoulders, exposing the neckline, which was low cut in front with either a curved or a straight edge. The revers were brought down into a V-opening to the waist, sometimes the opening descending below the waistline. The new fashion often had the collar and cuffs of a matching fur. The V-shape was either laced across the kirtle bodice, or a stomacher was inserted.

The sleeves were usually of three types: the wide funnel shape which allowed the bottom edge to fall downwards to the hem line (1450–1460); the loose-fitting style which was cylindrical to the wrist and often edged with fur (1450–1470); and the close-fitting style which came to the knuckles or had large turned-back cuffs (1460 to 1520). The belt or girdle was usually very wide, embroidered and worn tight to the waist.

By the 1470s the bodice was fitted closer to the body in a moulded fashion to the waist, sometimes to hip level. From there the skirt extended to fall to the ground in full natural folds, often with a long train. The bodice was fastened either down the front or the back. Also, during this period, the bodice and skirt of the gown were frequently joined together by a seam at the waist. Sometimes this type of gown reached only to the knees, revealing the skirt of the under-garment, the kirtle, which trailed to the ground. The neckline was cut very low, the front edge rounded up to a short point at the centre. Surrounding the neckline was a flat, drooping collar, often of fur, which always matched the cuffs. The collar broadened out over the shoulders and came below the upcurved point of the neckline in the centre front. The sleeves for this style followed the previous fashion. The girdle or belt was now more narrow and was worn looser either round the waist or hips, often with a long, dangling end. The belt, if worn, was usually made of metal discs of small plaques. With the low-necked, houppelande-gown fashion a 'fill-in' of soft, white material arranged in folds crossed the shoulders in a V-shape both in the front and at the back. This was often called a 'gorget' or 'neckerchief'.

For the wealthier, jewelled necklaces or throat collars were worn.

GOWN
Towards the end of the century the loose gown came into fashion. This gown had a square neckline which revealed the bodice of the close-fitting under-garment, the kirtle, or

The high-waisted, small-bodice fashion. The neckline was rounded and fairly low cut with narrow collars of fabric or fur. The skirt was full and hung in heavy folds to the ground. The hem of the skirt was often ornamented with a band of fur. The hair was combed back from the face, the forehead and eyebrows being plucked. The flowerpot headdress was decorated in diverse ways, stiffened with wire or gauze and set at various angles. This style was called the 'butterfly headdress' (c. 1484).

The roll headdress known as 'heart-shaped', curved low over the forehead in a sharp U-shape, and was decorated with jewels (c. 1460).

Middle-class fashion of the shaped headdress with a short veil at the back (c.1451).

gorget. It was fastened down either at the front where it was almost concealed, or the bodice was laced across the V-shaped opening in the front, both often being laced from behind. Sometimes the gown was allowed to hang loose from the shoulders, but usually the bodice was close fitting. The skirts were always very full and had trains. The trains were usually long and hitched up and fastened to the girdle at the back. If no girdle was worn, the train was fastened to the back of the gown by a brooch. Often the train was draped and carried over one arm, and was always richly lined. When the train was carried, the lining was decoratively displayed. The sleeves for this fashion were wide and large at the wrist.

The sideless surcoat, although worn, was at this period mainly used for ceremonial purposes and continued to be used in this capacity until 1520. Mantles continued to be worn unchanged throughout the century.

HEADDRESS AND HAIR

All head-gear, towards the end of the fifteenth century, was high and worn towards the back of the head. The fashion of the shaven forehead and plucked eyebrows continued. The ears were left uncovered and exposed. The curious fashion of a U-shaped loop of material in the centre of the forehead was a very common characteristic in about 1480. The sausage-shaped padded roll continued in fashion, now becoming more oval and elongated in shape (1440–1485).

The *turkey bonnet* or *chimney-pot* style of head-wear with a veil attached to the top which could be looped round the chin or allowed to hang behind, was very popular from 1460 to 1480. The horned head-dress lost much of its popularity when the French style of pointed, steeple-shaped *hennin* came into vogue. This fashion was very short-lived in England and the English modification of the truncated cone, which was a cut-off version of the French hennin, became popular. The truncated cone resembled the shape of an inverted flowerpot and stood no higher than 22 cm and was worn at an angle of 40 degrees. To enable the wearer to adjust to this somewhat cumbersome headdress, a black velvet frontlet, or small loop, was attached to the centre front. This truncated hennin was covered with a long veil which was allowed to hang down the back, sometimes reaching the ground, and was either attached over the top or draped over the centre of the hennin. In the same way as the train, this veil was often carried over one arm (1460–1480). After 1470 a broad band of black material was attached over the front of the hennin, the ends hanging down either side of the face, to about shoulder level.

The *butterfly headdress* was very popular during the second half of the century, but less fashionable after 1485. This headdress was made of transparent gauze placed over a wire frame which in turn was built over a small, embroidered, flowerpot hennin. This was placed on the back of the head and enclosed the hair. The wire frame was shaped to a V-shaped dip in the centre over the forehead. Often the gauze was arranged low over the forehead (1450–1495). This headdress was at first worn at much the same angle as the hennin, but later it was placed more horizontally. The veil was worn in a similar manner to the front piece of material on the hennin, or was pinned to the centre front, radiating back on several wires. A shortened version of the hennin later became the 'bonnet' style of the Tudor period.

Towards the end of the fifteenth century veils became narrower and longer, the ends being knotted to prevent them trailing on the ground.

The turban style headdress with a short veil and a follybell trimming worn around the collar of the décolletage (c. 1457).

FOOTWEAR

Stockings and hose remained unchanged generally throughout the period. Shoe styles and fashions followed the male modes, but women's shoes were never piked. The buskins were only worn when travelling. Pattens with short, pointed toes had cross straps over the instep but had no heel support.

ACCESSORIES

Dress accessories remained fairly constant, following the fashion of the earlier part of the century. During the Lancastrian and Yorkist period, the roses, both red and white, were greatly used for decorative motifs.

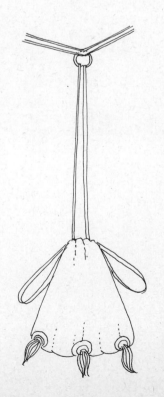

Woman's bag worn on a girdle.

Glossary

Aiglet	Metal tags attached to the ends of laces or ribbons.
Bagpipe Sleeves	Long, wide sleeves, tight to the wrists. The huge hanging pouch was often used as a pocket.
Baldrick	Jewelled shoulder belt.
Barbette	French term for a piece of material draped under the chin and pinned to the hair either side of the head.
Base	Jacket or jerkin with a deep skirt hanging in tubular pleats.
Bliaud	Long, close-fitting tunic, slit up the sides for riding.
Braies	Loose fitting drawers, sometimes worn to the ankle in the eleventh century, were tied by a running string. Later they became shorter to the knees.
Braiers	French equivalent of braie girdle, for pulling in the waist of braies and tying in the front.
Breeches	Upper part of long hose which were then combined in the form of tights. The upper part often became a different colour and material in the sixteenth century.
Burlet	Circular, padded roll. Part of the chaperon.
Buskins	High boots in various designs reaching up to the knees.
Butterfly headdress	Wired framed headdress supporting a veil above the head with a V-shaped dip over the forehead and spreading out like wings on either side, attached to a small ornamental cap.
Caul	Also known as a crespine. A head covering in a heavy net or reticulated gold or silver and jewelled. Similar to a fret.
Chainse	Body garment usually made of linen.
Chaperon	Type of hood with a liripipe, either twisted up on a burlet or left hanging.
Chaplet	Garland of flowers or ribbons worn around the head.
Chasuble	Long sleeveless cloak with a head opening.

Chemise	Under-garment of soft material, usually in a saffron colour.
Chiton	Originally Greek, a rectangular piece of wool or linen sewn up the sides and fastened at the shoulders by fibulae. Worn long for women and shorter for men.
Cod-piece	Small bag that concealed the opening of men's breeches, sometimes used as a pocket.
Coif	Plain, close-fitting linen cap.
Cote	Loose everyday tunic worn by both male and female.
Cote-hardie	Close-fitting, knee-length over-garment buttoned down the front. A low neckline and elbow length sleeves with extensions. After about 1350 it was shortened and sleeve extensions lengthened to tippets, which were often dagged.
Covrechief	Norman term for headrail.
Cowl	Hood attached to a cape.
Cracowes	Piked shoes.
Crespine or *Crespinette*	Net similar to a caul, shaped like a bag and made of gold, silver or silk, with jewels at the intersections.
Dagging	Slashings on borders as a form of decoration. Introduced 1346.
Doublet	Padded jacket, close fitting and waisted, worn next to the shirt.
Epaulettes	Ornamental shoulder tabs.
Estaches	Strings to attach hose to the gipon.
Fibula	Ancient Roman pin or brooch resembling the present-day safety-pin.
Fillet	Narrow band tied round the hair. It was also a stiffened circlet of linen worn with a barbette or fret.
Fitchet	French term for vertical placket pocket in a side seam.
Follybells	Decorative bells suspended in chains from the girdle, baldrick, or neckband.
Fouriaux	Silk sheaths usually in white with red circular stripes enclosing plaits.
Fret	Type of skull cap or coif in a trellis-work design made of metal.
Garde-corps	Voluminous super-tunic with long, wide sleeves and hood, worn in winter without a belt.
Garnache	Long, loose super-tunic with cape-like sleeves hanging over the shoulders, cut in one with the body, sometimes left open at the sides. The neck opening had two small, tongue-shaped lapels at the neck, usually of a paler colour.
Gipon	Close-fitting, padded, waisted garment to knee level in the early fourteenth century. Later it became shorter, closing down the front with lacing or buttons and long, tight sleeves which buttoned on the outer side to the elbow.

Goffering	Fluting or ruffles in small pleats, made with a goffering iron.
Gorget	Cape part of the hood or chaperon, similar to a wimple.
Gown	A long, loose, upper-garment varying in design, usually with wide or hanging sleeves.
Grande-assiette Sleeves	Worn on the gipon, cut circular to overlap the front and back of body.
Gypcière	Large three-tasselled draw purse attached to waist by a strap.
Headrail	Saxon term for a head-dress from the fifth to eleventh centuries. Made of cotton or linen, it was wide enough to drape the shoulders, completely covering the hair, and was held in place by either a crown or fillet.
Herigaud	Three-quarter to full length gown with full hanging sleeves.
Hennin	Steeple-shaped head-dress.
Horned headdress	Headdress with wide templers wired to resemble horns with a veil hanging down behind.
Houppelande	Voluminous upper gown falling in tubular folds from the shoulders to ground or thigh length. The sleeves were usually very wide.
Huke	Short over-garment similar to a tabard, sometimes with sleeves and usually worn with a belt.
Jacket	Short body garment. After 1450 worn as an upper-garment.
Jerkin	Jacket worn over a doublet, sometimes with hanging sleeves.
Kirtle	Saxon origin. A type of under-garment like a petticoat worn by both sexes.
Knightly girdle	Decorative belt made of metal clasps joined together, closing at the front with an ornamental buckle. Always worn at hip level by the nobility over the gipon or cote-hardie.
Liripipe	Long, hanging part of a chaperon or hood.
Page-boy hair style	Shoulder length hair, the ends turned under.
Palla	Rectangular shawl-like wrap worn in the Roman era by men, women and children.
Pattens	Overshoes made generally of wood, secured by leather straps. They were worn on boots or shoes to keep them clean from the dirty roads.
Pedestrian tabard	Ground-length type of huke with a waist girdle or just the front panel tied with a belt, and the back panel allowed to fall freely.
Petticoat	Later known as a waistcoat. An under-garment like a doublet, padded and worn for warmth.
Phrygian bonnet	In Roman times made of felt or leather, fastening under the chin, an emblem of liberty.
Pikes	Shoes with long points extending beyond the toes.
Pelisson	Super-tunic or over-gown lined with fur.
Plackard	Front panel or stomacher often embroidered or fur-trimmed.

Points	Ties tipped with metal ends.
Pokys	Same as bagpipe sleeves.
Poulaines	Long, pointed shoes.
Pourpoint	Same as a doublet.
Roc	Saxon name for a super-tunic.
Sideless surcoat	Low-necked, sleeveless over-garment, open at the sides from shoulder to hips. The sleeves and bodice of the garment beneath were visible.
Stola	Long, straight robe worn with short set-in sleeves by women in the Roman era.
Stomacher	Front chest covering the gap of a low-cut garment, often decorated.
Super-tunic	Loose garment placed over the head and worn over the tunic with wide sleeves, also named 'surcoat' or 'surcote' in the fourteenth and fifteenth centuries, but closer fitting in the fourteenth century.
Surcote	Same as a super-tunic.
Tabard	Medium-length circular mantle, similar to a garnache.
Templers	Ornamental metal bosses enclosing the hair either side of the face, supported by a connecting fillet or head-dress.
Tippet	Originally the long pendant of a hood, or hanging streamers from the sleeves of the cote-hardie.
Toga	Usually a semi-circular wrap revealing only the right arm.
Tunic	Loose body garment of different lengths, similar to a kirtle or cote.
Turkey bonnet	Tall, cylindrical hat without a brim.
Wimple	Piece of material draped under the chin and pinned to the hair on either side of the head.

Bibliography

Asser, Joyce, *Historic Hairdressing* Pitman 1966
Barfoot, A., *Everyday Costume in England* Batsford 1961
Black & Garland, *History of Fashion* Orbis 1975
Boehn, Max von, *Modes & Manners* (8 vols) Harrap 1926
Boucher, F., *20,000 Years of Fashion* Abrams
Bradfield, N., *Historical Costumes of England* Harrap 1958
Brooke, Iris, *English Costume in the Early Middle Ages* A. & C. Black 1964
——, *English Costume in the Late Middle Ages* A. & C. Black 1964
——, *History of English Costume* Methuen 1937
——, *Medieval Theatre Costume* A. & C. Black 1967
Calthrop, D. C., *English Costume* A. & C. Black 1906
Cooke, P. C., *English Costume* Gallery Press 1968
Courtais, G. de, *Womens Headdress & Hairstyles* Batsford 1973
Cunnington, P., *Costume in Pictures* Studio Vista 1964
——, *Handbook of English Medieval Costume* Faber & Faber 1954
Embleton, G., *Saxon England* Almark 1975
Gorsline, D., *What People Wore* Bonanza 1951
Hansen, H., *Costume Cavalcade* Methuen 1956
Hope, Thomas, *Costumes of the Greeks & Romans* Constable 1962
Kelly, Mary, *On English Costume* Deane 1934
Koehler, C., *History of Costumes* Constable 1963
Laver, James, *Concise History of Costume* Thames & Hudson 1969
——, *Costume* Batsford 1956
——, *Costume through the Ages* Thames & Hudson 1964
Lister, Margot, *Costume* Herbert Jenkins 1967
——, *Costume of Everyday Life* Barrie & Jenkins
Ruppert, J., *Le Costume – Antiquite – Moyen Age* Flammarion 1930
Truman, N., *Historic Costuming* Pitman 1936
Wilcox, R. R., *The Mode in costume* Scribner's 1942
Wilson, E., *History of Shoe Fashion* Pitman 1969
Yarwood, D., *English Costume* Batsford 1952
——, *Outline of English Costume* Batsford 1967
Pictorial Encyclopedia of Fashion Hamlyn 1968

Index